The Library at Warwick School
Please return or renew on or before the last date below

3/14

The History of Modern China

Zhiyue Bo, Ph.D.

Mason Crest
Philadelphia

CHINA
THE EMERGING SUPERPOWER

The History of Modern China

Zhiyue Bo, Ph.D.

Mason Crest
Philadelphia

Mason Crest
370 Reed Road
Broomall, PA 19008
www.masoncrest.com

Copyright © 2013 by Mason Crest, an imprint of National Highlights, Inc.
All rights reserved.
Printed and bound in the United States of America.

CPSIA Compliance Information: Batch #CH2013-9.
For further information, contact Mason Crest at 1-866-MCP-Book.

First printing

1 3 5 7 9 8 6 4 2

Library of Congress Cataloging-in-Publication Data

Bo, Zhiyue.
  The history of modern China / Zhiyue Bo.
      p. cm. — (China : the emerging superpower)
  Includes bibliographical references and index.
  ISBN 978-1-4222-2162-4 (hardcover)
  ISBN 978-1-4222-2173-0 (pbk.)
  ISBN 978-1-4222-9451-2 (ebook)
  1. China—History—19th century—Juvenile literature. 2. China—History—20th century—Juvenile
literature. 3. China—History—2002-   —Juvenile literature. I. Title.
  DS755.B63 2012
  951—dc22
                                2010047751

Table of Contents

Introduction

Dr. Jianwei Wang
University of Wisconsin–Stevens Point

Before his first official visit to the United States in December 2003, Chinese premier Wen Jiabao granted a lengthy interview to the *Washington Post*. In that interview, he observed: "If I can speak very honestly and in a straightforward manner, I would say the understanding of China by some Americans is not as good as the Chinese people's understanding of the United States." Needless to say, Mr. Wen was making a sweeping generalization. From my personal experience and observation, some Americans understand China at least as well as some Chinese understand the United States. But overall there remains some truth in Mr. Wen's remarks. For example, if you visited a typical high school in China, you would probably find that students there know more about the United States than their American counterparts know about China. For one thing, most Chinese teenagers start learning English in high school, while only a very small fraction of American high school students will learn Chinese.

In a sense, the knowledge gap between Americans and Chinese about each other is understandable. For the Chinese, the United States is the most important foreign country, representing not just the most developed economy, unrivaled military might, and the most advanced science and technology, but also a very attractive political and value system, which many Chinese admire. But for Americans, China is merely one of many foreign countries. As citizens of the world's sole superpower, Americans naturally feel less compelled to learn from others. The Communist nature of the Chinese polity also gives many Americans pause. This gap of interest in and motivation to learn about the other side could be easily detected by the mere fact that every year tens of thousands of Chinese young men and women apply for a visa to study in the United States. Many of them decide to stay in this country. In comparison, many fewer Americans want to study in China, let alone live in that remote land.

Nevertheless, for better or worse, China is becoming more and more important to the United States, not just politically and economically, but also culturally. Most notably, the size of the Chinese population in the United States has increased steadily. China-made goods as well as Chinese food have become a part of most Americans' daily life. China is now the second-largest trade partner of the United States and will be a huge market for American goods and services. China is also one of the largest creditors, with about $1 trillion in U.S. government securities. Internationally China could either help or hinder American foreign policy in the United Nations, on issues ranging from North Korea to non-proliferation of weapons of mass destruction. In the last century, misperception of this vast country cost the United States dearly in the Korean War and the Vietnam War. On the issue of Taiwan, China and the United States may once again embark on a collision course if both sides are not careful in handling the dispute. Simply put, the state of U.S.-China relations may well shape the future not just for Americans and Chinese, but for the world at large as well.

The purpose of this series, therefore, is to help high school students form an accurate, comprehensive, and balanced understanding of China, past and present, good and bad, success and failure, potential and limit, and culture and state. At least three major images will emerge from various volumes in this series.

First is the image of traditional China. China has the longest continuous civilization in the world. Thousands of years of history produced a rich and sophisticated cultural heritage that still influences today's China. While this ancient civilization is admired and appreciated by many Chinese as well as foreigners, it can also be heavy baggage that makes progress in China difficult and often very costly. This could partially explain why China, once the most advanced country in the world, fell behind during modern times. Foreign encroachment and domestic trouble often plunged this ancient nation into turmoil and war. National rejuvenation and restoration of the historical greatness is still considered the most important mission for the Chinese people today.

Second is the image of Mao's China. The establishment of the People's Republic of China in 1949 marked a new era in this war-torn land. Initially the Communist regime was quite popular and achieved significant accomplishments by bringing order and stability back to Chinese society. When Mao declared that the "Chinese people stood up" at Tiananmen Square, "the sick man of East Asia" indeed reemerged on the world stage as a united and independent power. Unfortunately, Mao soon plunged the country into endless political campaigns that climaxed in the disastrous Cultural Revolution. China slipped further into political suppression, diplomatic isolation, economic backwardness, and cultural stagnation.

Third is the image of China under reform. Mao's era came to an abrupt end after his death in 1976. Guided by Deng Xiaoping's farsighted and courageous policy of reform and openness, China has experienced earth-shaking changes in the last quarter century. With the adoption of a market economy, in just two decades China transformed itself into a global economic powerhouse. China has also become a full-fledged member of the international community, as exemplified by its return to the United Nations and its accession to the World Trade Organization. Although China is far from being democratic as measured by Western standards, overall it is now a more humane place to live, and the Chinese people have begun to enjoy unprecedented freedom in a wide range of social domains.

These three images of China, strikingly different, are closely related with one another. A more sophisticated and balanced perception of China needs to take into consideration all three images and the process of their evolution from one to another, thus acknowledging the great progress China has made while being fully aware that it still has a long way to go. In my daily contact with Americans, I quite often find that their views of China are based on the image of traditional China and of China under Mao—they either discount or are unaware of the dramatic changes that have taken place. Hopefully this series will allow its readers to observe the following realities about China.

First, China is not black and white, but rather—like the United States—complex and full of contradictions. For such a vast country, one or two negative stories in the media often do not represent the whole picture. Surely the economic reforms have reduced many old problems, but they have also created many new problems. Not all of these problems, however, necessarily prove the guilt of the Communist system. Rather, they may be the result of the very reforms the government has been implementing and of the painful transition from one system to another. Those who would view China through a single lens will never fully grasp the complexity of that country.

Second, China is not static. Changes are taking place in China every day. Anyone who lived through Mao's period can attest to how big the changes have been. Every time I return to China, I discover something new. Some things have changed for the better, others for the worse. The point I want to make is that today's China is a very dynamic society. But the development in China has its own pace and logic. The momentum of changes comes largely from within rather than from without. Americans can facilitate but not dictate such changes.

Third, China is neither a paradise nor a hell. Economically China is still a developing country with a very low per capita GDP because of its huge population. As the Chinese premier put it, China may take another 100 years to catch up with the United States. China's political system remains authoritarian and can be repressive and arbitrary. Chinese people still do not have as much freedom as American people enjoy, particularly when it comes to expressing opposition to the government. So China is certainly not an ideal society, as its leaders used to believe (or at least declare). Yet the Chinese people as a whole are much better off today than they were 25 years ago, both economically and politically. Chinese authorities were fond of telling the Chinese people that Americans lived in an abyss of misery. Now every Chinese knows that this is nonsense. It is equally ridiculous to think of the Chinese in a similar way.

Finally, China is both different from and similar to the United States. It is true that the two countries differ greatly in terms of political and social systems and cultural tradition. But it is also true that China's program of reform and openness has made these two societies much more similar. China is largely imitating the United States in many aspects. One can easily detect the convergence of the two societies in terms of popular culture, values, and lifestyle by walking on the streets of Chinese cities like Shanghai. With ever-growing economic and other functional interactions, the two countries have also become increasingly interdependent. That said, it is naïve to expect that China will become another United States. Even if China becomes a democracy one day, these two great nations may still not see eye to eye on many issues.

Understanding an ancient civilization and a gigantic country such as China is always a challenge. If this series kindles readers' interest in China and provides them with systematic information and thoughtful perspectives, thus assisting their formation of an informed and realistic image of this fascinating country, I am sure the authors of this series will feel much rewarded.

A view of downtown Hong Kong, 1997. On July 1 of that year, Great Britain returned Hong Kong to China after more than 150 years of colonial rule—an event that to many Chinese symbolized the start of a new era in China's history.

Overview: A Historic Day

Torrential rains fell on the island of Hong Kong during the evening of June 30, 1997, but the deluge did not prevent a massive pyrotechnic display. Between 8:00 and 8:30 P.M. local time, some 25,000 fireworks were sent skyward from three barges in the middle of Victoria Harbour. Through the rain, each explosion released a ball of shimmering color. Six large maroon fireworks marked the finale, the loud clap of their detonation reverberating for several moments off Hong Kong's steel-and-glass skyscrapers. Then, as a witness later recalled, "all was quiet, aside from the sound of cheers and applause floating across the harbour."

As the cheers and applause in Hong Kong subsided, farther north, in the Chinese capital of Beijing, a large, festive crowd was assembling in historic Tiananmen

Square. Much attention was focused on the two-story digital clock whose red numbers were counting down by seconds. By the time the fireworks concluded in Hong Kong, about three and a half hours remained on the clock display.

Back in Hong Kong, a banquet began in the island-city's Convention Centre. Among the approximately 4,000 guests in attendance were a host of diplomats, foreign ministers, and former heads of state. But the major roles were reserved for Chinese and British officials. On the Chinese side these officials included President Jiang Zemin and Premier Li Peng. On the British side were Charles, Prince of Wales; Prime Minister Tony Blair; and Chris Patten, who for the past five years had served as governor of Hong Kong.

Just before midnight the Union Jack, Great Britain's familiar red, white, and blue flag, was lowered, along with the flag of Hong Kong, which consisted of a small Union Jack, a dragon, and a lion. In their place, just after midnight on July 1, were raised the red and yellow flag of the People's Republic of China, as well as a new flag for the Hong Kong Special Administrative Region, consisting of a white flower on a red field.

In Beijing, the crowd in Tiananmen Square erupted into a raucous celebration. In Hong Kong, however, a few more acts of pomp and circumstance had to be attended to. With a band playing "Rule Britannia," Prince Charles, Chris Patten, and other British dignitaries boarded the royal yacht *Britannia*. Accompanied by a small flotilla of British naval vessels, the yacht sailed out of Victoria Harbour toward the South China Sea, with the ships' guns firing a thunderous salute before they disappeared from view. At that, Hong Kong residents commenced what officials billed as "the party of the century."

The reason for the celebration—as well as the ceremonies that preceded it—was an event of historic significance. As of midnight on July 1, 1997, Hong Kong Island—located south of China's Guangdong Province—was again a part of China, having been

The flag of Hong Kong (right) flies next to the Chinese flag at Victoria Park.

returned by Great Britain after more than 155 years of colonial rule. In addition to Hong Kong Island, the British returned the two other parts of their Hong Kong colony: Kowloon Peninsula, to the north of the island, and the New Territories, consisting of some 235 islands and area on the mainland, north of Kowloon. Britain had forced a defeated and humiliated China to cede or lease the three sections composing the Hong Kong colony in three unequal treaties signed during the 19th century, beginning with the 1842 Treaty of Nanjing. This ushered in a long period of decline during which China, a great nation with a recorded history of 4,000 years, suffered domination at the hands of foreign powers.

But by the mid-1900s, following the defeat of the Japanese in World War II, China began to reemerge as an important country. The 1997 British handover of Hong Kong, along with the December 1999 return of Macao by Portugal, signaled the culmination of this process. By the the early years of the 21st century, China had taken its place as one of the most powerful nations in the world.

The ruins of St. Paul's Cathedral in Macao, built in 1602, is a symbol of centuries of European colonial rule or influence in China. Macao was a Portuguese colony from the 1550s until control was returned to the Chinese government in 1999.

The Middle Kingdom Humbled by the West

At the end of the 18th century, China was the wealthiest and most productive country in the world. In 1800 China produced one-third of the world's total manufacturing output—more than that of all countries in the West combined. China's pride in cultural terms was also vividly conveyed in the country's name in Chinese, *Zhongguo*, meaning Middle Kingdom (reflecting the view that China was the center of the civilized world and was surrounded by barbarians). Only a few years earlier, in 1793, the emperor of the Middle Kingdom, Qianlong, had issued two edicts to King George III of Great Britain, admonishing him not to pursue diplomatic relations or seek to extend trade with China. On the one hand, the edict declared, it was "utterly impracticable" for the Middle Kingdom to grant every nation of Europe diplomatic residence in Beijing;

and on the other hand, the Middle Kingdom possessed all things and saw no value in strange or ingenious objects.

Within half a century, however, the Middle Kingdom would be forced to interact with the West. And in the process, China would surrender its sovereignty over trade and territories, and lose a substantial portion of its pride as well.

The Opium War

The first clash between China and the West was over opium, an addictive narcotic drug. Because of its adverse effects on the health of the Chinese population, opium was prohibited under several 18th-century emperors of the Qing dynasty, a dynasty established by Manchu conquerors in 1644. Nevertheless, opium trade grew rapidly in the 1830s. Emperor Daoguang, who reigned from 1821 to 1850, decided to end the illicit trade once and for all. He appointed Lin Zexu (1785–1850), a Fujian scholar-official, as a special imperial commissioner and sent him to Guangzhou (Canton), the capital of Guangdong Province and the only port open to foreign trade, to put an end to opium trafficking.

Upon his arrival at Guangzhou on March 10, 1839, Commissioner Lin urged drug dealers, Chinese and foreign, to surrender their possessions and to sign a bond pledging not to engage in the illicit traffic in the future. Captain Charles Elliot, the British superintendent of trade in China, surrendered 21,306 chests of opium on behalf of the British smugglers but refused to comply with Lin's demand to sign the bond. Instead, he asked London to start "prompt and vigorous proceedings" against China. The British foreign minister, Lord Palmerston, without prior consultation with Parliament, informed Elliot that the government of Britain had decided to send an expeditionary force to China.

Fighting began on November 13, 1839, when the Chinese navy, seeking to protect British traders who had signed the bond in defiance

During a 1793 mission to Beijing on behalf of King George III, British diplomat Sir John Barrow made this colored drawing of a Chinese town, titled *Wall of the City of Yang-teheou-foo*. Britain's initial attempts to establish a trade relationship with China were rebuffed by the emperor.

of Elliot's order, engaged a British warship. But the Opium War did not officially begin until January 31, 1840, when the Indian government declared war on China on behalf of the British Crown.

British reinforcements arrived in China in June 1840. The expeditionary force consisted of 16 warships mounting 540 guns, four armed steamers, 27 transports, one troop ship, and 4,000 soldiers. It was under the leadership of Rear Admiral George Elliot, cousin of Captain Elliot. Instead of attacking China from Guangzhou, which Commissioner Lin had been prepared to defend, the British fleet blockaded the entrance to the harbor and sailed north. Under a white flag, Admiral Elliot and Captain Elliot were attempting to deliver a letter from Lord Palmerston to "the Minister of the Emperor of China" on July 2 at Xiamen (Amoy). The Chinese, however, fired at them, apparently having no idea what a white flag meant in a military conflict. After their second attempt at Ningbo, the two Elliots finally delivered the letter to Governor-General Qishan near Tianjin, on August 29. With the British forces threatening Beijing, the emperor dismissed Lin and appointed Qishan imperial commissioner.

Qishan persuaded the British to leave the north for Guangzhou, where he would meet them for negotiations. Under military threat, however, Qishan was forced into a convention at Chuanbi, near Guangzhou, in January 1841. According to the convention, China would cede Hong Kong Island to Britain and pay the British an indemnity of 6 million Mexican silver dollars (the widely circulated currency at the time). Enraged by Qishan's unauthorized agreement, the emperor recalled him in chains.

Lord Palmerston was equally furious with Charles Elliot for not exacting better terms for the British. He fired Elliot and appointed Sir Henry Pottinger as the new plenipotentiary (representative with full power) to deal with China. He instructed Pottinger to make a new agreement with the emperor himself.

Pottinger arrived in China in August 1841. Under his leadership, the British fleet captured Xiamen, Ningbo, and Zhoushan. With reinforcements from India in spring 1842, Pottinger launched a campaign against major cities along the coast. The British took Shanghai in June and Zhenjiang in July, blocking the traffic on the Grand Canal and lower Yangzi (Yangtze) River. The Grand Canal was a lifeline for the Qing court over which grains were shipped to northern China. The occupation of Zhenjiang cut this lifeline, and concerned provincial officials requested that the emperor permit peace negotiations. Ignoring Qing requests for peace talks, Pottinger pushed on to Nanjing (Nanking), the former Ming dynasty capital, and took up attack positions outside the city walls in August. The Qing quickly sued for peace. The Treaty of Nanjing, drafted in English and translated into Chinese, was signed by

Henry Pottinger and three Chinese plenipotentiaries on August 29, 1842, aboard a British warship moored in the Yangzi River.

The Treaty of Nanjing and the Treaty System

The Treaty of Nanjing contained 13 articles with significant ramifications for China's sovereignty. According to the treaty, the Qing government agreed to: 1) pay the British government an indemnity of $21 million; 2) open five ports—Guangzhou, Fuzhou, Xiamen, Ningbo, and Shanghai—to trade and residence for British subjects and their families, and allow British consulates to be established in these cities; and 3) cede the island of Hong Kong to Britain.

Imposed as it was by the victor upon the vanquished at gunpoint, the Treaty of Nanjing was perhaps bound to be an unequal agreement. But the disadvantageous position China found itself in was exacerbated by the Chinese delegates' inexperience with Western diplomatic interactions. The Chinese delegates insisted on trivial distinctions in terminology while giving up important rights. For example, they were adamant that in the Chinese text a word meaning "granting with benevolence" be used in the article on opening the five ports to foreign trade and residence, but they failed to negotiate the terms of foreign presence on China's soil.

In a subsequent treaty, the Treaty of the Bogue, signed on October 18, 1843, the Chinese delegates agreed to a fixed import duty of 5 percent on average and to a fixed export duty of 1.5 percent to 10.5 percent; allowed British consuls to subject their citizens to British laws instead of Chinese laws (extraterritoriality); allowed British ships to anchor at the five ports to protect commerce and control sailors; and gave Britain most-favored-nation status, whereby China would grant Britain whatever rights that might be conceded to other powers later.

Partly because of their ignorance of international law and partly because of their traditional policy of playing off the "barbarians" against one another, the Chinese granted similar rights to the Americans and the French. In the Treaty of Wangxia (Wangsia), signed on July 13, 1844, the Chinese agreed to most-favored-nation status for the United States, extraterritoriality for American citizens in China, the Americans' rights to maintain churches and hospitals in the five ports, and treaty revision in 12 years. It was in this treaty that prohibition of the opium trade—the original cause of the war with Britain—was finally specified. On October 24, 1844, the Chinese signed the Treaty of Huangpu (Whampoa) with France, granting the French the right to propagate Catholicism in the five ports.

From the perspective of the Chinese, none of these articles seemed to be vitally injurious. Granting the most-favored-nation treatment was an indication that the emperor looked upon people from afar

Chinese soldiers armed with clubs and wicker shields, 1860. The Chinese were no match for modern European armies, and during the 19th century China's rulers were forced to sign a series of one-sided treaties.

with equal benevolence; extraterritoriality was expedient because it was better to allow barbarians, who spoke unintelligible languages and had strange customs, to govern themselves; and the fixed tariff rate of 5 percent was higher than the existing imperial tariff of 2 to 4 percent. Once agreed upon, however, these stipulations severely restricted China's sovereignty. Most-favored-nation treatment allowed all Western countries to benefit, without the need to negotiate directly with the Chinese government, from any concession made by the Chinese government to any other country. With extraterritoriality, China gave up its legal rights over disputes on Chinese territory. By agreeing to a fixed tariff rate, China lost the ability to adjust tariffs in the future. And all the individual treaties, taken together, formed a treaty system, pushing China, the Middle Kingdom, toward a semi-colonial status without the knowledge of Chinese officials.

Foreign Encroachment and New Treaty Settlement

To the British merchants, the short-term commercial results of the Treaty of Nanjing were disappointing. The five treaty ports were open, but trade was intolerably slow. By 1850 there were only 19 adult foreigners living in Ningbo and 10 in Fuzhou. Trade out of Xiamen was not much better, except for traffic in Chinese laborers to work in the sugar plantations of Cuba. Guangzhou, the city where the whole conflict had started originally, was practically closed to foreigners because of local resistance. Only Shanghai, a city located on the east coast of China near the mouth of the Yangzi River, offered any hope of commercial profits. There, one could find more than 100 merchants.

Dissatisfied with their limited access to the Chinese market, the British, applying the most-favored-nation clause to the American treaty of 1844 that had requested a renewal of the treaty in 12 years, demanded a revision of the Treaty of Nanjing. In addition to market access, the British, along with the French and the

Americans, also demanded legalization of the opium trade, abolition of interior transit taxes, and establishment of diplomatic residence in Beijing.

Taking advantage of the *Arrow* incident, in which the British flag aboard a ship was allegedly "insulted," the British recommenced military actions at Guangzhou in 1856. The French, capitalizing on the murder of a missionary in February 1856 in Guangxi Province (which was not open to the West then), soon joined the British. The Anglo-French forces took over the city of Guangzhou on December 28, 1857, capturing the governor-general of Guangdong and Guangxi. After the allied forces had taken the strategic Dagu forts and Tianjin in May 1858, the Qing court hurried two imperial commissioners with "full power" to Tianjin for negotiations. Ultimately the negotiations resulted in four treaties of Tianjin: one with Russia (June 13), one with the United States (June 18), one with Britain (June 26), and one with France (June 27).

According to these treaties, China would open 10 new ports; permit foreign travel anywhere in China with valid passports, and foreign travel without passports within 33 miles of the treaty ports; fix interior transit taxes at 2.5 percent; allow Christian missionaries to preach in all parts of China; and pay an indemnity of 4 million taels of silver for Britain and 2 million taels for France. Most devastatingly, the imperial commissioners agreed to allow a British ambassador to reside in Beijing, something the Qing court had been trying to avoid since 1793. Moreover, because of most-favored-nation agreements, China had to extend the same privileges of diplomatic residence in Beijing to all other countries.

Under pressure from the emperor, the Chinese imperial commissioner persuaded the British to locate their diplomatic residence in Shanghai, some 800 miles away from Beijing. After their unsuccessful attempt to block Frederick Bruce, the British envoy, from going to Beijing to exchange the treaty ratifications in May 1859, the Chinese asked him to take the tributary route. (This was the route traveled by emissaries of states paying tribute to the Chinese emperor.) Bruce, however, insisted on taking the imperial route to Beijing, which had been deliberately blockaded with iron spikes, chains, and solid rafts. When the British forces tried to clear the obstructions on the imperial route, against Chinese warnings, they were attacked and repulsed.

Reinforcements from Britain and France arrived in China in August 1860 and charged all the way to Beijing. On October 18, the British burned the Yuan Ming Yuan (Garden of Perfect Brightness), the 139-year-old Summer Palace, to the ground. The emperor had fled the city for Rehe (Jehol), Manchuria, and left his younger brother, Prince Gong, behind for the peace settlement. On the very day the Summer Palace was destroyed, Prince Gong reaffirmed the terms of the 1858 Treaty of Tianjin. Without any negotiations, he also accepted all the terms of a new treaty, the Convention of Beijing. With this new treaty, Britain increased its indemnity from 4 million to 8 million taels; acquired Kowloon Peninsula, opposite Hong Kong Island; and established its diplomatic residence in Beijing. The French and the Russians also secured separate treaties with China, advancing their interests in the country. By the extension of the most-favored-nation treatment, other countries would also receive similar privileges. Consequently, these treaties, along with the first set signed after the Opium War, formed a colonial trap from which China would not escape for the next 84 years.

其九 東端林平

勇ある我東端
其刀を揮ふを
流電の如く一人
四騎と闘ふて
人馬共る斫る

This illustration from a Japanese book depicts a mounted Chinese soldier being cut down by a Japanese swordsman. China's humiliating defeat in the Sino-Japanese War of 1894–1895 started a period of social and governmental reform.

3

Self-Strengthening and Other Reform Efforts

In the aftermath of the 1860 Convention of Beijing, Prince Gong emerged as an important leader. In the eyes of the Chinese, the prince was a hero because he had been able to send the barbarians away without the support of an army or a navy. Under his leadership, China began to adopt a set of reform measures intended to revitalize the Chinese empire. The decades-long effort, known as the Self-Strengthening Movement, focused on the adoption of Western diplomatic practices and Western military and industrial innovations.

Diplomatic reform, the first phase of the Self-Strengthening Movement, began with recommendations that Prince Gong and Grand Councilor Wenxiang issued on January 11, 1861. Following these recommendations, China soon established a new office, the Zongli Yamen, to deal with foreign affairs; created a new post, superintendent of trade, in Tianjin to take charge of the three northern ports (another superintendent of trade, stationed in Shanghai, was responsible for the original five ports); and established a new school, the Tongwen Guan (School of Common Languages), in Beijing to instruct select boys from elite Manchu families in foreign languages. Another measure of diplomatic reform, interestingly enough, was to appoint a British man as inspector-general of customs with the duty to collect tariffs for the Chinese government and to supervise the Maritime Custom Service, a Chinese agency staffed exclusively by foreign employees.

In the meantime, Prince Gong and Grand Councilor Wenxiang—as well as a number of provincial leaders, such as Zeng Guofan, Li Hongzhang, and Zuo Zongtang—also pursued military modernization projects. Prince Gong and Grand Councilor Wenxiang recognized that the Chinese defeats of the previous two decades were due primarily to the Western forces' more advanced arms and equipment. The most urgent task, then, was to acquire Western ships and guns.

China's first attempt at military modernization, however, turned out to be a fiasco. In 1862 Prince Gong commissioned Horatio Lay, then inspector-general of customs, to purchase and equip a steam fleet. Lay bought eight ships and hired Captain Sherard Osborn of the British Royal Navy as the commander-in-chief of the fleet. According to an agreement signed in England with Lay, Osborn was to accept orders only from the Chinese emperor via Lay. When the fleet arrived in Shanghai in September 1863, however, Captain Osborn was told to report to provincial authorities as an assistant commander-in-chief. Osborn protested on the basis of his agreement with Lay, yet the

Zongli Yamen refused to change its position. After weeks of inconclusive negotiations, the Zongli Yamen decided to disband the fleet. Osborn was paid a lump-sum fee of 10,000 taels and sent home; Lay was given £14,000 and dismissed as inspector-general of customs. In all, the Chinese government had spent £550,000 on acquiring a modern navy, but in the end it had nothing to show for the outlay.

In contrast, projects under the sponsorship of provincial authorities went much more smoothly. Zeng Guofan (1811–1872), the governor-general of Liangjiang responsible for the provinces of Jiangsu, Anhui, and Jiangxi, built the Jiangnan Arsenal at Shanghai in 1865. Zuo Zongtang (1812–1885), governor-general of Zhejiang and Fujian, established the Fuzhou Dockyard in 1866. And Li Hongzhang (1823–1901), the most influential figure of the Self-Strengthening Movement, sponsored the Nanjing Arsenal (1867), the China Merchants' Navigation Company (1872), a naval academy (1880) and a military academy (1885) at Tianjin, and the Beiyang Fleet (1888).

After the death of Zeng Guofan in 1872, the Self-Strengthening Movement shifted into its second phase: industrialization. Under the sponsorship of Li Hongzhang, China constructed telegraph lines; built railways; and established a series of modern enterprises such as the Kaiping Coal Mines (1877), the Shanghai Cotton Cloth Mill (1878), and the Mohe Gold Mines (1887). Other provincial authorities also followed suit in sponsoring industrial enterprises.

As a result of these efforts in the Self-Strengthening Movement, the Chinese government became accessible to foreign diplomats and merchants; China developed its capacity to produce guns, ships, and industrial products; and China's military power was substantially boosted. Whether China had fully caught up with foreign powers remained to be seen.

Sino-Japanese War of 1894–1895

The first major test of China's progress came from a nation that, during the Ming period (1368–1643), had been one of its tributary states. Japan had entered a period of rapid modernization following the reestablishment of imperial rule (the Meiji Restoration) in 1868. Soon it began to cultivate territorial ambitions in East Asia, seeking opportunities to expand on the Asian mainland after the fashion of Western imperialism. Japanese leaders fixed their gaze on Korea.

A leading tributary state of China during both the Ming and Qing periods, Korea had for centuries maintained intimate relations with its larger neighbor and relied on China for protection from foreign (especially Japanese) invasion. By the 1870s, however, Japan had begun to challenge China's position in Korea. In 1894, when a secret religious group called the Tonghak (Eastern Learning) rebelled against the Korean king, China intervened to help the Korean court. After the Chinese had suppressed the rebellion, the Japanese responded by dispatching 8,000 troops of their own to Korea. With a confrontation looming, Li Hongzhang, the Chinese official in charge of Korean affairs, belatedly sent reinforcements to Korea. On July 25, 1894, the Japanese navy sank a ship carrying these reinforcements, the steamer *Gaosheng*, in the Korea Bay. About 950 Chinese soldiers drowned, and on August 1, China and Japan declared war on each other.

Though outnumbered, the Japanese quickly smashed the Chinese forces. On land, the Japanese dealt a fatal blow to Li's army at Pyongyang. At sea, the Japanese sank four Chinese ships in one battle. Most embarrassingly for the Chinese, the Japanese managed to take the Chinese forts and turn Chinese guns on Chinese ships. In March 1895 the Chinese sued for peace. After more than 30 years of "self-strengthening," China had suffered another crushing defeat.

This 1895 illustration shows Japanese forces overrunning the Chinese defenders at the Liao River port city of Newchwang (Yingkou), in Manchuria.

The Treaty of Shimonoseki, signed in April 1895, imposed humiliating terms on China. According to the treaty, China would have to recognize Korean independence; pay an indemnity of 200 million taels to Japan; cede Taiwan, the Pescadores, and the Liaodong Peninsula to Japan; open the ports of Chongqing, Suzhou, Hangzhou, and Shashi to trade; and grant Japanese nationals rights to open factories and engage in industry and manufacturing in China. Later, with the intervention of Russia, France, and Germany, China was able to keep the Liaodong Peninsula—but only at the cost of an additional 30 million taels. These treaty terms completely destroyed the financial health of the Qing government, whose annual revenue stood at only 89 million taels.

One Hundred Days' Reforms of 1898

At the outset of the Sino-Japanese War, most military observers had predicted a quick victory for the Chinese. In retrospect, however, it is

An Ill-Fated Reign

Guangxu, the Qing dynasty's second-to-last emperor, ascended to the throne in 1875, upon the death of Emperor Tongzhi. But because Guangxu was only four years old at the time, his aunt, Dowager Empress Cixi (widow of Emperor Xianfeng and mother of Tongzhi), ruled as regent. When Guangxu was ready to assume his full duties as China's emperor in 1889, the dowager empress retired to the Summer Palace, northwest of Beijing. Behind the scenes, however, she continued as China's actual ruler.

In 1898, in the midst of his efforts to reform China's government, educational system, and economy, Emperor Guangxu came into conflict with the dowager empress. After several weeks of tension, she acted decisively. Emerging from the Summer Palace with an army of supporters, Cixi entered the Forbidden City and seized the 27-year-old emperor, placing him under house arrest.

For the next 10 years, Emperor Guangxu remained a prisoner of his aunt. On November 14, 1908, he died mysteriously, aged 37. Some historians believe that he was poisoned by Cixi because she wished to name his successor before her death (she chose Guangxu's two-year-old nephew Puyi, who would reign as China's last emperor). The dowager empress died on November 15, 1908, the day after Guangxu's death.

easy to see the reasons for China's defeat. While Japan brought the full weight of its modernized military forces to bear in the conflict, China used only a part of its available forces—namely, Li Hongzhang's Huai Army and Beiyang Fleet. For self-preservation, China's other fleet, the Nanyang Fleet, and two provincial squadrons at Guangzhou and Fuzhou remained neutral throughout the war. China's problems had been compounded by the Qing court's misuse of naval funds for the reconstruction of the Summer Palace and by rampant corruption in Li's army and fleet.

The repercussions of the defeat were profound in China, especially among intellectuals. Two scholars, Kang Youwei (1858–1927) and his student Liang Qichao (1873–1929), wrote a 10,000-word memorial (a statement of facts accompanied by a petition) to the emperor and gathered the signatures of 603 intellectuals from different provinces. These intellectuals, who had originally gone to Beijing for national examinations, protested the peace treaty and urged the throne to initiate institutional reform. Their memorial, however, failed to reach the emperor largely because of its blunt language and emotion.

Undeterred, Kang continued to petition the emperor, who finally received his third memorial, of May 29, 1895. Impressed by the memorial, Emperor Guangxu (1871–1908) ordered that copies be made for Dowager Empress Cixi, the Grand Council, and provincial authorities. Although Kang was not of sufficient rank to qualify for an audience with the emperor, Guangxu ordered that he be interviewed by high officials of the Zongli Yamen and that in the future he be allowed to present his memorials without obstruction.

The reform program undertaken by Emperor Guangxu (pictured here) was blocked by his advisers and by his powerful aunt, Dowager Empress Cixi.

Under Kang's influence, Emperor Guangxu decided to launch a comprehensive program of reforms. Between June 11 and September 20, 1898, he issued more than 40 edicts, urging changes in the areas of education, government administration, industry, and international cultural exchange. In the area of education, he called for essays on current affairs to replace the old-fashioned (or "eight-legged") essays of the civil service examinations; for the establishment of an Imperial University at Beijing as well as modern schools in the provinces; and for the publication of an official newspaper. In public administration, he urged abolition of unnecessary offices, establishment of a dozen new bureaus in the Zongli Yamen, improvement in administrative efficiency, and encouragement of suggestions from private citizens. In industry, he promoted railway construction and the development of agriculture, manufacturing, and commerce. He also suggested that high officials tour foreign countries, that legal codes be simplified, and that a national budget be prepared.

Although the emperor made a few personnel changes in order to push through his reforms, his program was blocked by most of the high officials in the central and provincial administrations. The Board of Rites, which was in charge of the civil service examinations, strongly opposed the abolition of the eight-legged essay. The Zongli Yamen frowned upon the proposal to create 12 new bureaus.

Dowager Empress Cixi (1835–1908) ruled China as regent before the accession of Guangxu, and again after his imprisonment in 1898.

And—most seriously as it turned out—Guangxu's reforms ultimately ran afoul of Dowager Empress Cixi.

Though she had officially retired to the Summer Palace in 1889, the dowager empress—Guangxu's aunt—retained tremendous power. Initially she seemed amenable to the emperor's program. As the reform progressed, however, she became alarmed. Increasingly, it appears, she saw the reforms as a scheme by which the emperor was trying to wrest power from her. A confrontation seemed inevitable, and in September 1898, Beijing was rife with rumors that the emperor would soon be deposed.

Perhaps fearing for his safety, Emperor Guangxu rejected a request that he and the dowager review troops at Tianjin in October. But on September 16 the emperor gave an audience to Yuan Shikai (1859–1916), a military leader with a new army of 7,000 men near Tianjin. During the audience, the emperor praised Yuan's accomplishments and granted him a promotion.

Two days later Yuan was approached by a reformer and ally of the emperor, Tan Sitong (1865–1898). Fearing an impending coup against the emperor, Tan urged Yuan to kill Ronglu, a Manchu general and confidant of the dowager empress, and to besiege the Summer Palace. During a second audience with Yuan on September 20, the emperor seemed to offer another promotion upon Yuan's completion of this mission. But Yuan divulged the plot to Ronglu on his return to Tianjin that afternoon. On September 21, Dowager Empress Cixi returned to the Forbidden City, the imperial palace complex in Beijing, and placed the emperor under house arrest.

Six important reformers, including Tan Sitong and Kang Guangren (Kang Youwei's younger brother), were rounded up and decapitated. With that, the reforms of 1898 came to a tragic and premature end, after a scant 103 days.

Xuantong, also known as Puyi (1906–1967), sits next to his father, Prince Chun. The infant became China's last emperor in 1908, the same year this photo was taken. Four years later he abdicated the throne, paving the way for the establishment of the Republic of China.

4

Fall of the Qing and the Struggle for Control

In the late 19th century, following the Sino-Japanese War, foreign imperialists added to their territorial and monetary gains in the previous half-century by further carving up China into leased territories and spheres of influence. Germany occupied the port of Qingdao in Shandong Province and, in 1898, forced the Qing government to agree to a 99-year lease on Jiaozhou (Kiaochow), an area of about 200 square miles that included Qingdao. Britain took over the harbor at Weihaiwei on the north of the Shandong Peninsula, and in 1898 the British leased from the Qing a territory north of Kowloon (later known as the New Territories) for a period of 99 years. Russia moved into Manchuria and occupied Lüshun (Port Arthur).

France claimed special rights in the southern and southwestern provinces of Yunnan, Guangxi, and Guangdong, and on the island of Hainan. And Japan, after its occupation of Taiwan, continued its penetration of the mainland. The United States, a latecomer, urged an "open door" policy for China so that it could share the spoils with other imperialists.

The Boxer Uprising

Under these circumstances, strong anti-foreign sentiment was fermenting in both the imperial court and in Chinese society at large. Frustrated with the intensified foreign imperialism, Dowager Empress Cixi and her advisers decided to take action. With their encouragement, the Boxers—originally an anti-Qing secret society—rose to avenge the national humiliations of the previous six decades. Known as "Yi He Quan" (Righteous and Harmonious Fists) in Chinese, the Boxers preferred fists (as well as swords and lances) to guns because of the latter's foreign origin. As men and women of magic power, they claimed immunity to bullets. They burned churches and foreign residences in Beijing and Tianjin and killed foreign missionaries and Chinese Christians in Shanxi, Henan, Hebei, Inner Mongolia, and Manchuria.

After the dowager issued a declaration of war on June 21, 1900, however, a foreign expeditionary force of 21,000 troops, consisting of soldiers from Japan, Russia, Britain, the United States, France, Austria, Italy, and Germany, arrived at Dagu in late July and set out on August 4 from Tianjin to Beijing. The Boxers, mostly still shunning the use of guns, turned out not to be immune to bullets. Many of them were killed as the allied forces charged all the way to Beijing within 10 days. The dowager fled the next morning in disguise for Xi'an (the capital of Shaanxi Province) along with the emperor, who had originally wanted to stay for peace talks. In Beijing some of the allied forces went on a spree of wanton violence and destruction,

(Left) A Chinese man with a spear and shield holds the flag of the Boxer Rebellion. (Below) International troops assemble in the Forbidden City.

burning palaces, looting treasures, killing soldiers and civilians alike, and raping Chinese women.

After much debate among themselves, the representatives of the allies, later swollen to 11 countries, forced the Qing's representatives, Li Hongzhang and Prince Qing, into a peace treaty, the Boxer Protocol, on September 7, 1901. According to the treaty, China would punish high officials involved in the Boxer uprising; forbid imports of arms for two years; destroy the Dagu and other forts from Beijing to the sea; allow foreign troops to be stationed in 12 strategic points from Beijing to the sea; suspend official examinations for five years in 45 cities where the Boxers had been active; make the Zongli Yamen into a Ministry of Foreign Affairs as the premier office of the

Qing government; send apology missions to Germany and Japan; allow permanent foreign guards to protect the legation quarters in Beijing; and pay an indemnity of 450 million taels over 39 years, at an annual interest rate of 4 percent. The total payment, including both the principal and the interest, exceeded 982 million taels, more than all the indemnities of the previous 60 years combined.

The 1911 Revolution

Clearly, the Qing government was decadent beyond repair. As if to repeat the 1894–1895 debacle, the modernized Qing armies had mostly remained out of the conflict; those that did participate in the fight proved ineffective, and the southeastern provincial authorities protected foreign lives and property and suppressed the Boxers within their jurisdictions.

Although the Qing court was once again searching for ways to recuperate, a revolutionary movement aiming to overthrow the Qing was emerging under the leadership of Dr. Sun Zhongshan (Sun Yat-sen). Educated in the United States and Hong Kong, Dr. Sun (1866–1925) was interested less in medicine than in revolution. Disgusted with the Qing's defeat by the French in 1884–1885 over Annam (now Vietnam) and disappointed at the Qing's loss in the Sino-Japanese War of 1894–1895, he was determined to "expel the Manchus, restore China, and establish a republic." He organized the Revive China Society in 1894 and formed the Chinese Revolutionary Alliance in 1905.

After 10 unsuccessful military uprisings in the south and the southwest, Sun's followers scored a major victory at Wuhan, in central China, in October 1911. From there the revolution spread rapidly, and by the end of November two-thirds of China's provinces had declared themselves independent of Qing rule. On January 1, 1912, Sun Zhongshan was inaugurated as the provisional president of the new Republic of China.

Sun would not lead the republic for long. As the revolution had begun to spread from Wuhan, the anxious Qing court—now under the reign of a five-year-old boy emperor, with his aunt serving as regent—had asked the military leader Yuan Shikai for help. Yuan proceeded to take advantage of the Qing court's weakness and the revolutionaries' inexperience. After arranging for the abdication, in 1912, of Emperor Xuantong (1906–1967)—and thus putting an end to the Qing dynasty after 267 years—Yuan brushed Sun aside and made himself provisional president of the Republic of China. Sun, who lacked the military forces to contest the issue, could only watch from Nanjing while his rival ruled from Beijing. But Yuan's appetite for power proved insatiable. As a provisional

Dr. Sun Zhongshan (1866–1925) led a revolutionary movement that replaced imperial rule with a republican form of government. Unfortunately, he was soon pushed aside by Yuan Shikai, whose grasping for more and more power helped plunge China into a period of warlordism.

president, he wanted to be a president. As a president, he wanted to have unlimited 10-year terms. As a life-long president, he wanted to become an emperor. His push for more and more power eventually alienated even his supporters, and in early 1916 he was forced to abandon his short-lived reign as emperor. A few months later he died.

Warlordism, the CCP, and the GMD

After the death of Yuan Shikai, China disintegrated into a period of warlordism. Warlords controlled different areas of the country, ranging from one to several provinces, and fought with one another

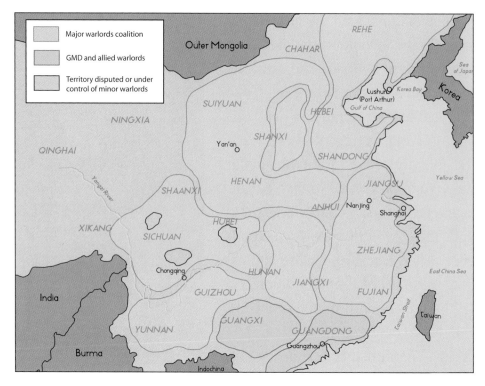

This map shows China in 1925, before the Northern Expedition. The combined Guomindang–Chinese Communist Party campaign against the warlords successfully extended central government control over much of the country.

over dominance of the central government as well as over one another's territories.

In the midst of this chaos, two important political parties were coming together: the Chinese Communist Party (CCP) and the Guomindang (GMD), referred to in previous years as the Kuomintang, or KMT. The CCP was a product of international and domestic developments in the late 1910s. Internationally, the success of the Russian Revolution in 1917 brought hope for a social revolution along Communist lines in China. Domestically, an anti-imperialist mass demonstration on May 4, 1919 (later known as the May Fourth Movement), provided impetus for such a revolution. In July 1921 the founding meeting of the CCP was held secretly at a girl's boarding school in the French Concession of Shanghai. The meeting, attended by 12 delegates representing 57 members, had been organized by two professors of Beijing University under the advice of agents of the Communist International (Comintern, for short).

In the meantime, Sun Zhongshan, after his failures to carry the Chinese republican revolution forward, was also contemplating a reorganization of the GMD (known in English as the Nationalist Party, though this is a misnomer) after the fashion of the Soviet Communist Party. At his meeting with Sun, the Dutch agent of the Comintern, H. Maring, proposed a merger of the CCP and the GMD with the latter as the basis. The CCP reluctantly passed a resolution in August 1922 to permit individual Communists to enter the GMD, while Sun gladly embraced the idea of mobilizing workers and peasants through CCP members and utilizing Soviet aid in his course of national revolution. Sun also adopted the Comintern's suggestion for establishing an army of his own and sent Jiang Jieshi (Chiang Kai-shek, 1887–1975) to Moscow for three months to study the Soviet military system.

The first National Congress of the GMD was held January 20–30, 1924, with 165 delegates in attendance. The Huangpu (Whampoa) Military Academy, near Guangzhou, was soon established in June with Jiang Jieshi as its president.

After the death of Sun Zhongshan on March 12, 1925, the GMD-CCP alliance conducted the Northern Expedition to wipe out the warlords. The National Revolutionary army, consisting of 6,000 Huangpu cadets and 85,000 troops, set out on July 27, 1926, on its campaign against the northern warlords Wu Peifu, Zhang Zuolin, and Sun Chuanfang. Under the leadership of Jiang Jieshi, the revolutionary army conquered the southern half of the country within nine months, taking Wuhan in September, Nanchang in November, Fuzhou in December, and Nanjing in March of the following year. It was at Nanjing that Jiang set up a Guomindang government.

Guomindang troops, 1920s. After taking Shanghai in 1927, Jiang Jieshi turned against his erstwhile Communist allies, sparking two decades of intermittent GMD-CCP civil war.

After Jiang entered Shanghai in March 1927, however, he openly split with the CCP. On April 12 Jiang's forces moved against CCP members and their sympathizers. His troops and secret agents raided CCP cells, shot suspects on sight, disarmed the workers' pickets, and eliminated the labor unions in Shanghai, Nanjing, Hangzhou, Fuzhou, Guangdong, and other places.

After several unsuccessful military uprisings in Nanchang, Changsha, and Guangzhou, the CCP went underground. One of the CCP units, under the leadership of Mao Zedong (Mao Tse-tung, 1893–1976), retreated to Jinggangshan, a border area of Jiangxi and Hunan Provinces. Later joined by the forces under Zhu De (1886–1976) and Peng Dehuai (1898–1974), Mao expanded his army and revolutionary bases with land reform policies and guerrilla military tactics. Started in September 1927 with fewer than 1,000 soldiers, the Red Army of the CCP grew quickly. By October

1930 it claimed 40,000 soldiers and was in control of 34 counties with a combined population of 2 million.

Jiang Jieshi, who was increasingly concerned with the expansion of CCP forces, began a series of military campaigns against the Red Army in December 1930. His plan was to encircle and then exterminate the Communists. Even though his forces far outnumbered the Red Army and were directed by well-trained military professionals with German advisers, Jiang failed in three successive campaigns, the last in September 1931. Under the leadership of Mao and Zhu, the Communists thwarted Jiang's army with flexible guerrilla tactics.

While Jiang focused on annihilating the Communists in the south, the Japanese set their sights on acquiring Chinese territory farther north. After its victory in the 1904–1905 Russo-Japanese War, Japan had replaced Russia as the principal foreign power in Manchuria, a region in northeastern China. The Japanese maintained an army there, supposedly for the protection of their country's trade interests. On September 18, 1931, a bomb blew up a section of track along the Japanese-operated Southern Manchurian Railway; it was probably planted by Japanese troops. In any case, Japan used the incident as a pretext for conquering Manchuria and setting up a puppet government there.

Instead of resisting the Japanese, Jiang decided to continue his fight against the CCP, believing that the Communists were the larger threat. Although his fourth campaign was not successful, his fifth campaign, which coincided with leadership changes in the CCP's revolutionary bases, proved quite effective. In the early 1930s the central leadership of the CCP, based primarily in Shanghai, was dominated by a group of Chinese Communists who had studied in the Soviet Union and were known as the Twenty-eight Bolsheviks. In January 1933 they moved from Shanghai to the revolutionary base areas.

Bo Gu (1907–1946), the CCP's main central leader, criticized Mao and hired a German-born Comintern agent as his military adviser. Unfortunately, that adviser—Otto Braun, who was also known as Li De (1900–1974)—had no idea of the local topography and directed the troops according to a map. For his part, Bo was unfamiliar with military affairs and espoused a vague strategy of "punching the enemy with both fists."

The shortcomings of Bo and Li proved costly when Jiang Jieshi assembled half a million troops and launched his largest military campaign against the Communists. The Red Army suffered major casualties and lost all revolutionary base areas in Jiangxi Province. Forced from Ruijin, Jiangxi Province, where it had thrived in the previous seven years, the Red Army in October 1934 began what came to be known as the Long March. Altogether there were about 86,000 CCP soldiers and officials when this epic trek started.

Mao, who had been under the criticism of the CCP's Provisional Politburo (Political Bureau) since November 1931, was still without military power at the beginning of the Long March. Under the direction of Bo Gu and Li De, the CCP troops managed to break Jiang's encirclement within 45 days, but the troops were reduced to 30,000. Jiang set up four lines of defense with 200,000 troops in the north, but Bo and Li insisted on marching in that direction. Knowing about Jiang's plans, Mao proposed to go west, the direction where Jiang had the fewest troops. With support from Zhou Enlai (Chou En-lai, 1898–1976), another central military leader, Mao's proposal was adopted and the Red Army avoided another major blunder.

In January 1935, when the Red Army took Zunyi, Guizhou Province, the CCP held an enlarged Politburo meeting with 20 participants. At the meeting, Bo Gu and Li De were criticized for their mistakes and Mao was elected a standing member of the Politburo. A few days later, Mao was appointed an assistant to Zhou in military

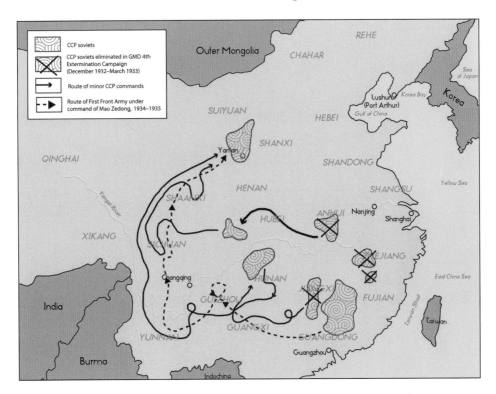

This map shows the route of the Long March. The epic retreat from Jiangxi Province to Shaanxi Province covered some 7,500 miles and firmly established Mao Zedong as the preeminent Chinese Communist Party leader.

affairs. Later, under Mao's suggestion, a new three-man group on military affairs was established, with Mao and Wang Jiaxiang as members and Zhou as the leader. Zhou, who respected Mao's military experience and resourcefulness, gladly deferred to Mao in commanding the CCP troops.

Under the leadership of Mao, the Red Army eventually escaped Jiang's trap. In October 1935 the survivors reached the safety of Shaanxi Province in North China. The Long March, a trek of 25,000 *li* (7,750 miles) across 11 provinces, was over. Of the 86,000 soldiers and officials who had begun the march a year before, only 8,000 remained. Nevertheless, the Red Army had survived.

Japanese troops enter a walled city in northern China, 1937. Throughout the 1930s the Japanese moved aggressively into Chinese territory, beginning with the 1931 invasion of Manchuria. The brutal fighting of the 1937–1945 Sino-Japanese war resulted in the deaths of an estimated 35 million Chinese.

5

Triumph of the Communists

As the 20th century unfolded, Japan's imperialist ambitions in China gradually surpassed those of the Western powers. Taking advantage of World War I in Europe, Japan declared war against Germany and invaded Jiaozhou, the German leasehold in Shandong Province, in 1914. The following year, Japan issued President Yuan Shikai an ultimatum of 21 demands, requesting wide-ranging imperialist rights in China. Through these demands, the Japanese wanted to control Shandong, Manchuria, Inner Mongolia, the southeast coast of China, and the Yangzi Valley, as well as China's policies in the areas of public administration, finance, military, and the police. Although Yuan accepted most of the demands under the Japanese threat, the Chinese legislature refused to ratify the treaty he had signed with the Japanese. Japan entered a series of secret treaties with

Russia, Britain, France, Italy, and the United States in 1917 to secure its special rights in China, but the formal transfer of German concessions in Shandong to Japan at the Paris Peace Conference triggered strong protests from China and led to the May Fourth Movement of 1919.

In the 1920s, Japanese militarists dreamed of creating a vast empire. They came to believe that "to conquer the world it is necessary to conquer China first, and to conquer China it is necessary to conquer Manchuria and Mongolia first." On September 18, 1931, a bomb exploded on the Southern Manchurian Railway track outside Shenyang (Mukden). The next morning the Guandong army—the Japanese army stationed in Manchuria since 1905—occupied Shenyang, claiming that the explosion had been an attack by Chinese soldiers and that it was acting in self-defense. Within three days the Japanese troops had taken Changchun, Andong, Yingkou, and Jilin.

Jiang Jieshi had instructed Zhang Xueliang (1901–2001), nicknamed "the Young Marshal," not to engage the Japanese; Zhang was effectively the ruler of Manchuria. A few days before the incident of September 18, Jiang had transferred the bulk of the northeastern forces at Shenyang. Unopposed, the Guandong army overran all of Manchuria in just four months. To legitimize their naked aggression, the Japanese created the puppet state of Manzhouguo (Manchukuo), meaning the state of Manchuria, on March 9, 1932, and installed Puyi, the last emperor of the Qing dynasty, as its puppet ruler.

After their occupation of Manchuria, the Japanese encroached upon the provinces of North China. They created the Eastern Hebei Autonomous Council in December 1935 and sponsored an autonomy movement for the five provinces of Hebei, Chahar, Suiyuan, Shanxi, and Shandong. More than any other country in the world, Japan posed a threat to the survival of the Chinese nation.

The Xi'an Incident and the Anti-Japanese Coalition

In the face of the intensified Japanese aggression, Jiang's policy of not fighting the Japanese was increasingly losing moral ground. Similarly, his continuing attacks on the CCP began to strike even GMD supporters as wrong. The CCP called for a unified front against Japanese imperialism, and its slogan "Chinese must not fight Chinese" resonated. Two commanders in Shaanxi, Zhang Xueliang and Yang Hucheng (1893–1949), balked at carrying out Jiang's order to exterminate CCP troops in the province. The CCP's calls for a united Chinese front against the Japanese held particular appeal for the Young Marshal, whose father had been murdered by the Japanese in 1928 and whose homeland of Manchuria had been occupied by the Japanese since 1931. When Jiang flew to Xi'an, the headquarters of Zhang and Yang, to supervise the campaign of extermination in person, a mutiny broke out on December 12, 1936. When Zhang's men found Jiang in a cave on the mountainside in the back of his residence, he told them that he was the Generalissimo. "Yes, Generalissimo," was the reply, "you are also a live captive."

Later on the morning of December 12, Zhang issued a circular telegram with a list of eight demands on Jiang: to reorganize his government into a broad coalition of all parties and groups for national salvation; to stop the civil war; to release patriotic leaders who had been arrested in Shanghai; to release all political prisoners elsewhere; to guarantee freedom of assembly; to encourage patriotic movements; to carry out the will of Sun Zhongshan faithfully; and to convene at once a National Salvation Conference. With Zhou Enlai's mediation as a representative of the CCP—which had modified its policy from "anti-Jiang and anti-Japan" to "ally with Jiang against Japan"—Jiang verbally agreed to the united front against Japan. Yet genuine cooperation between the GMD and CCP remained minimal.

In 1937 Japan renewed its aggression in China. On the pretext that a soldier was missing during a military exercise near the Marco Polo Bridge outside Beijing on July 7, 1937, the Japanese demanded to enter the nearby city of Wanping to conduct a search. When refused by the local Chinese garrison, the Japanese troops bombarded the city, beginning an all-out war against China. To destroy China's economic capacity for war, the Japanese opened a second front in Shanghai on August 13. With his capital, Nanjing, under immediate threat, Jiang issued a call for an all-out stand and rendered his endorsement for the united front publicly.

Burned and abandoned, a Chinese infant wails on a railroad platform in Shanghai moments after a Japanese air raid. Japan's invasion and occupation of China took a horrible toll on the Chinese people.

During World War II, Jiang Jieshi (1887–1975), better known in the West as Chiang Kai-shek, was designated the Allies' supreme commander in the Chinese theater and received much aid from the United States and the Soviet Union—including U.S. P-40 fighter planes, pictured below. Yet he failed to mount a significant campaign against the Japanese, probably because he was conserving resources for an eventual showdown with the CCP.

Jiang ordered his best German-trained troops—the 87th and 88th Divisions—to resist the Japanese in Shanghai at all costs, which they did heroically for three months. But the defense disintegrated when the Japanese made an amphibious landing at Hangzhou Bay, to the south of Shanghai. After taking Shanghai, the Japanese marched on to Nanjing. For sheer barbarity, what happened after the Japanese overcame the capital city's defenses has few parallels in world history. In a rampage that lasted nearly 11 weeks, the Japanese soldiers murdered indiscriminately—shooting, bayoneting, beheading, burning, and burying alive men, women, children, and babies—and raped tens of thousands of women and girls. By the time the reign of

> "The Japanese are a disease of the skin: it can be cured. The Communists are a disease of the soul: it affects the whole body."
>
> —Jiang Jieshi

terror—known notoriously as "the Rape of Nanking"—had ended, as many as 370,000 Chinese civilians and prisoners of war had been massacred and 80,000 women and girls raped.

The Eighth Route Army—the renamed and reorganized Red Army—won its first victory against the Japanese at Pingxingguan, in northeastern Shanxi Province, on September 25, 1937. In August 1940 it dealt another serious blow to the Japanese troops in North China in the Hundred-Regiments Offensive. But Jiang Jieshi feared the CCP's expansion. He had the New Fourth Army, the CCP force in South China, ambushed in January 1941 at Jing Xian, Anhui Province. After seven days of fighting, approximately 3,000 of the Communist troops were killed. After being captured, many more were shot or taken off to prison camps. Although the New Fourth Army was later allowed to reconstitute, intra-coalition frictions continued.

Chongqing, Yan'an, and the Anti-Japanese War

After the fall of Nanjing in December 1937 and Wuhan in October 1938, Jiang retreated to his new capital, Chongqing, Sichuan Province. Safe from the enemy because of its rugged terrain, precipitous gorges, and rapid currents in the narrowing Yangzi River, Chongqing was also isolated from the rest of the country. Though his government was recognized internationally as the only legitimate government of China, Jiang did not possess the strategic vision to lead the whole Chinese nation in a war against the Japanese. Nor did he have real command over all the military forces of China. But as a symbol of China's resistance, Jiang gained international attention and was the recipient of aid, most of it from the Allies fighting against Japan, Germany, and Italy in World War II. In January 1942, shortly after the Japanese attack on Pearl Harbor drew the United States into the Second World War, Jiang was made the Allies' supreme commander of the Chinese theater. Yet despite receiving financial, personnel, military, and diplomatic support from both the United States and the Soviet Union, he never mounted a concerted, effective challenge to the Japanese—in part, many historians believe, because he wanted to preserve his forces for a postwar struggle with the Communists.

Meanwhile, the CCP had established its headquarters in Yan'an, a poor, remote town in Shaanxi Province located about 500 miles north of Jiang's capital of Chongqing. In May and June of 1938, less than a year into the anti-Japanese war, Mao Zedong delivered a series of lectures in Yan'an on the nature of the conflict. In the lectures (which were later compiled as a book, *On Protracted War*), Mao predicted how the anti-Japanese war would play out. He envisioned a prolonged struggle that unfolded in three stages. The first stage would be the period of Japan's strategic offensive and China's strategic defensive; the second stage, the period of Japan's strategic consolidation and China's preparation for the counteroffensive; and the third stage, the period of China's strategic counteroffensive and Japan's strategic retreat. In the end, Mao confidently predicted, the Chinese people would triumph.

Mao Zedong's 10 Principles of War

In directing military campaigns against the Japanese and the GMD, foes who were better equipped and more numerous, Mao followed a strategy of guerrilla warfare based on 10 central rules.

1. Attack isolated enemy forces first; attack strong enemy forces later.
2. Take towns and rural areas first; take big cities later.
3. Wiping out the enemy's strength, not seizing territory, is the main objective.
4. Only attack enemy forces that can be completely overcome.
5. Fight no battle you are not sure of winning.
6. Have courage in battle and no fear of sacrifice or fatigue.
7. Attack the enemy when he is on the move.
8. In cities, seize all weakly defended battlements. Wait before attacking strong enemy lines.
9. Use captured arms and personnel to reinforce.
10. Rest, train, and consolidate in short intervals. The enemy should be permitted scant breathing space.

Under the leadership of Mao, the CCP and its armed forces expanded rapidly during this period. CCP membership increased from around 40,000 in 1937 to an estimated 800,000 in 1940. CCP forces grew from 29,000 regular soldiers in 1937 to 470,000 regular soldiers and 2.7 million militia members in 1944. In the

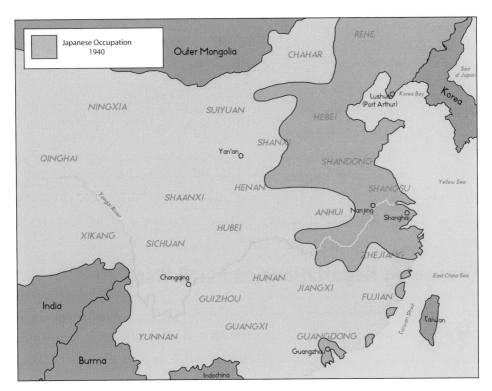

Although they conquered much of China's coastal region, the Japanese were unable to subdue China's vast interior.

meantime, Mao became the undisputed leader of the CCP: he was elected chairman of the Central Committee at the Seventh Party Congress in 1945, and Mao Zedong Thought (basically his views on applying and adapting the principles of communism to the situation in China) was written into the constitution of the CCP as the guideline for the whole party.

As Mao had predicted, the Japanese were forced to consolidate their early gains, after occupying Wuhan and Guangzhou in October 1938. Thereafter they were unable to subjugate China completely.

By the summer of 1945, Japan teetered on the brink of collapse after relentless bombing by the United States and the steady advance of U.S. forces toward the Japanese home islands. On

August 6 and 9, the United States dropped atomic bombs on the Japanese cities of Hiroshima and Nagasaki, respectively. A day before the Nagasaki bombing, the Soviet Union had declared war on Japan, and Soviet forces swept into Manchuria. Finally, on August 15, Emperor Hirohito announced Japan's unconditional surrender.

For China, this marked an important milestone: Japanese imperialism had finally been overcome. China had paid a terrible price on the road to victory, however. During their eight-year war with Japan, as many as 35 million Chinese had lost their lives.

Chongqing Negotiations and Civil War

If the war had led to an uneasy truce between the GMD and the CCP, the defeat of Japan signaled a resumption of Jiang's power struggle with the Communists. By war's end the Communists controlled large islands of territory, particularly in rural areas north of the Yangzi River. Jiang's forces were more concentrated in southern China.

Initially the factions jockeyed for advantage through diplomatic maneuvering. On August 14, 1945, Jiang sent the first of three telegrams inviting Mao Zedong to Chongqing for talks on national affairs. The GMD leader probably believed that Mao would decline the invitation out of fear for his safety—an outcome that would bolster Jiang's public image while making Mao seem uninterested in a peaceful resolution to China's political difficulties. But after giving the appearance that he would not attend the talks with Jiang, Mao surprised the GMD leader, and garnered good publicity on the world stage, by showing up in Chongqing on August 28.

Since Jiang was caught by surprise and largely unprepared for the talks, Mao presented his proposals first. Broadly, Mao wanted a free hand in areas that were then under the control of the CCP, including northern China, Inner Mongolia, and some important cities. He called for the convening of a political consultative conference, with participation by all political parties and groups; the legalization of all political parties; the release of all political prisoners; and the recognition of democratically elected governments. On the issue of the relative strength of the GMD and the CCP, he offered to keep 20 to 24 divisions if the GMD agreed to cut its forces to 120 divisions. On October 10, after 43 days of negotiations, Mao and Jiang issued a joint communiqué declaring their intention to support peaceful reconstruction of their country. Yet they failed to reach any substantive agreement.

Jiang had already decided to settle matters on the battlefield. On September 17, while the Chongqing negotiations were still in progress, he issued a secret order to exterminate the Communists. In October he launched an attack with 113 divisions and a total of 1.1 million troops.

U.S. president Harry Truman dispatched General George C. Marshall, the former chief of staff of the U.S. Army, to attempt to mediate an end to the civil war in China. In January 1946, after Jiang's initial attack had been repelled, Marshall succeeded in obtaining a cease-fire agreement between the GMD and the CCP. Unfortunately, the truce soon broke down, and fighting resumed in April.

Initially, Jiang's forces outnumbered Mao's by a ratio of five to one, and in December 1946 the GMD leader confidently predicted to Marshall that he would wipe out the Communists in 8 to 10 months. Mao, on the other hand, was predicting another protracted war of three to five years.

Between July and December 1946, Jiang's troops captured 165 towns and 67,000 square miles of territory from the Communists. In March 1947, they even took Yan'an, the CCP capital. But these gains spread Jiang's forces thin, and without the burden of protecting their territories the CCP troops had the flexibility to attack their enemy at the place and time of their choosing.

Mao Zedong proclaims the birth of the People's Republic of China, October 1, 1949. Pictured behind Mao in this painting are such prominent Communist leaders as Zhu De, Liu Shaoqi, and Zhou Enlai.

In July 1947 Mao's troops began their strategic offensive. Through three major military campaigns, the People's Liberation Army (PLA) defeated Jiang's 144 divisions of regular troops and 29 divisions of irregular troops. By early 1949 the remnants of Jiang's forces had withdrawn to a defensive line along the Yangzi River, leaving the Communists in full control of northern China, including Beijing.

Determined to eliminate the GMD and carry the Communist revolution to its very end, Mao ordered the PLA to cross the Yangzi River. This the PLA did on April 21. Two days later, the Communists occupied Nanjing, Jiang's capital. Soon GMD resistance had collapsed totally, and by the end of the year Jiang and several hundred thousand followers fled to the island of Taiwan. There Jiang claimed to preside over the legitimate government of China and, over the years, periodically announced his intention to reconquer the mainland. He served as president of the Republic of China until his death in 1975.

On October 1, 1949, the People's Republic of China (PRC) was founded in Beijing. On the occasion, Mao Zedong announced to the world that the Chinese people had finally stood up after having long been on their knees.

Mao Zedong casts his ballot in a 1953 People's Congress election. As chairman of the Chinese Communist Party, Mao ruled the People's Republic of China for 27 years.

6

Early Years of the People's Republic of China

As it consolidated power, the new Chinese government faced a variety of challenges. Years of warfare had wreaked havoc on production levels, and economic mismanagement by the Guomindang regime had exacerbated an already serious inflationary spiral. For example, a standard large sack of rice (weighing 171 pounds in Western equivalents) had been priced at 12 yuan in 1937, but it sold for 6.7 million yuan in early June 1948 and 63 million yuan in August of that year. Shopkeepers had to change their price cards several times daily as the value of the currency plunged.

Under the leadership of the CCP, the new government moved quickly to stabilize prices, curb inflation, and restore production. It controlled key commodities through state trading companies; removed money from circulation through taxes, bonds, and forced savings; reduced government expenditures; punished currency speculation; and encouraged production. As a result, the inflation rate was reduced to 15 percent by 1951, and by 1952 production had recovered to prewar levels in many spheres.

Land reform, something that Jiang's regime neglected, composed a large part of the CCP's program. As the Communists wrested control of territory in the countryside from the GMD, they redistributed land based on their experiences in Yan'an as well as in northern China and Manchuria. The land reform efforts continued after the founding of the People's Republic of China. Coordinated by work teams of 3 to 30 people each, the land reform proceeded in two steps: all village inhabitants were first categorized into different classes according to their landholdings; and then the land and other productive property of the landlord was confiscated and redistributed to all classes according to the size of the family. By the end of 1952, the CCP had redistributed 700 million *mu* (117 million acres) of land (about 43 percent of China's arable land) to 300 million peasants (about 60 percent of the rural population).

"Lean to One Side" Foreign Policy

The new government also adopted a new foreign policy, which Mao Zedong had enunciated even before the proclamation of the founding of the People's Republic of China. All Chinese, Mao declared in a June 1949 speech, "without exception must lean either to the side of imperialism or to the side of socialism. Sitting on the fence will not do, nor is there a third road."

In practical terms, what this meant was that in its foreign relations China would ally itself with the Soviet Union (with which it shared a socialist ideology), not the United States (a country Mao identified in his June 1949 speech as imperialist). The United States and the U.S.S.R., former allies in World War II, were embroiled in a global struggle for political dominance known as the Cold War, and—while he may have been open to some contacts with the United States—Mao had clearly decided to lean to the side of the Soviets.

In December 1949 Mao traveled to Moscow, where he met with Soviet leader Joseph Stalin. In February 1950 their negotiations culminated in the Treaty of Friendship, Alliance, and Mutual Assistance, which replaced the treaty that Stalin had signed with Jiang Jieshi in 1945. In addition, China received Soviet credits valued at U.S. $300 million.

The Korean War

The Sino-Soviet alliance alarmed U.S. policy makers, who saw the treaty as evidence of the formation of a monolithic Communist camp aligned against the United States. American anxieties were further heightened when, on June 25, 1950, troops from Communist North Korea invaded U.S.-supported South Korea across the 38th parallel, which formed the dividing line between the two regimes. The administration of U.S. president Harry Truman, pursuing a "containment" policy—that is, trying to prevent the spread of worldwide communism—quickly sent troops to aid the South Koreans; the United Nations Security Council (with the Soviet delegation absent) soon passed a resolution urging U.N. member states to oppose the North Korean aggression, and 16 countries contributed soldiers and other aid to help South Korea. The United States contributed the largest number of troops, and American officers were in overall command of the U.N. contingent.

On June 27 President Truman sent the U.S. Seventh Fleet to the Taiwan Strait to prevent the People's Republic of China from taking over Taiwan. Earlier in the year, stated American policy had been to remain neutral in the military conflict between the CCP and GMD forces, and the United States did not provide further aid to

A United Nations column retreats across the 38th parallel into South Korea ahead of the Chinese offensive that began along the Yalu River, 1950. The Korean War (1950–1953) brought U.S. and Chinese troops into direct combat with each other.

Jiang's troops. (Meanwhile, however, the United States had blocked attempts by the Soviet Union to take China's seat in the United Nations away from Taiwan and give it to the PRC.) On June 29 Premier Zhou Enlai protested the Seventh Fleet's presence in the Taiwan Strait, calling it "armed aggression against the territory of China." Zhou declared, "The fact that Taiwan is part of China will remain unchanged forever."

North Korea remained on the offensive throughout the early weeks of the Korean War; by early August the South Korean and U.S. troops were clinging to a small defensive perimeter around the southern city of Pusan, their last foothold on the peninsula. But on September 15, American troops landed behind North Korean lines at Inchon, and the North Korean front collapsed. In only two weeks the North Koreans had been pushed back to the 38th parallel.

Although China signaled that it might intervene in the war if the United States did not break off the allied offensive at the 38th parallel—Zhou Enlai warned that the PRC would not remain on the sidelines as "the imperialists wantonly invade the territory of [North] Korea"—South Korean, U.S., and United Nations units crossed the 38th parallel in early October. Mao secretly decided to commit Chinese troops to help the North Koreans.

In late October Chinese forces clashed with United Nations troops approaching the Yalu River, which forms the border between North Korea and China. Surprised, General Douglas MacArthur, supreme commander of the U.N. forces in Korea, pulled back. But MacArthur ordered the resumption of the offensive later in the month, after intelligence estimates placed the number of North Korean troops at about 80,000, and the number of Chinese troops between 40,000 and 80,000. In reality, about 850,000 Chinese troops were massed north of the Yalu, and on the evening of November 25, more than 300,000 of them swung into action. Overwhelmed, the American and U.N. troops began a long and sometimes chaotic retreat. The Communist advance was finally halted in January 1951, but not before Seoul, South Korea's capital, had fallen. A U.N. counteroffensive slowly pushed the Communist forces back, and by June the front stood roughly at the 38th parallel, where the two sides fought to a bloody stalemate over the next two years before the signing of an armistice in July 1953.

For the Chinese, the Korean War represented a victory, as they had prevented a potential American occupation of the entire Korean Peninsula, which would have presented major strategic difficulties for China; Mao had even feared that the United States might launch an invasion across the Yalu River and attempt to overthrow the government of the People's Republic of China. Of course, in forestalling that possibility, China had paid a heavy price: according to official Chinese statistics, about 150,000 Chinese soldiers lost their lives during the Korean War (Western estimates place the number considerably higher). In contrast, U.S. dead numbered fewer than 37,000.

Another outcome of the conflict on the Korean Peninsula was a hardening of U.S. policies toward the People's Republic of China. In December of 1950 the United States announced a total trade embargo on the PRC, a measure that would remain in place for more than two decades, and signed a mutual defense treaty with Taiwan that pledged U.S. support in the event of an attack by the PRC. The following May, Assistant Secretary of State Dean Rusk enunciated U.S. policy toward Taiwan and the People's Republic of China. "The regime in [Beijing] . . . is not the government of China," Rusk said. ". . . We recognize the national government of the Republic of China, [which will] . . . continue to receive important aid and assistance from the United States." As with the trade embargo, the United States would not officially recognize the PRC until the 1970s.

Political Transition and Socialist Transformation

American concerns about a monolithic Communist camp notwithstanding, there were significant differences between communism in the Soviet Union and communism in the People's Republic of China, and cracks in the two countries' relationship would begin to emerge by the late 1950s.

In spite of their ideological similarities, the Chinese Communist revolution and the Russian Revolution took dramatically different routes. In Russia the revolution succeeded in major cities first and then spread to the rest of the country, whereas the Chinese Communist revolution started in rural areas and then succeeded in major cities.

Moreover, the political, social, and economic structures of the PRC initially differed from those of the Soviet Union. Politically, the government of the Soviet Union was dominated by Communist Party members, while the government of the PRC was a coalition government of all social classes. In the early years of the PRC, the Chinese People's Political Consultative Conference (CPPCC) was the legislative organ of the PRC, pending the establishment of the National People's Congress; and the "Common Program" of the CPPCC served as a temporary constitution, pending a formal constitution. In China, out of six vice presidents, three were non-Communists; out of four vice premiers, two were non-Communists; out of 21 members of the Government Administrative Council (or cabinet), 11 were non-Communists; and out of 93 leaders in the central government, 42 were non-Communists.

Economically, the Soviet economy was based on state-owned enterprises and collective farms. The Chinese economy, on the other hand, consisted of five sectors: the state-owned sector, the cooperative sector, the private capitalist sector, the individual sector, and the state-capitalist sector (in which the state and private capitalists worked jointly).

Although the CCP, especially Mao Zedong, had had serious differences with the Soviet Communist Party over the direction of the Chinese Communist revolution between the 1920s and 1940s, the CCP of the 1950s was more willing to follow the example of the Soviet Union. For instance, the CCP had originally planned to keep the political, social, and economic structure that existed in 1949 for 10 to 20 years. Under the advice of Stalin, however, the CCP leadership decided to accelerate the pace of the political transition and the economic transformation (to socialism). The first meeting of the National People's Congress (NPC), a one-chamber body, was convened in September 1954; the NPC adopted the first constitution of the PRC and elected a new government.

As a result, the political structure in China became more similar to that in the Soviet Union. First, there was a dual system of the Party and the government at almost every level. At the central level, the decision-maker was the Politburo of the CCP, especially its Standing Committee; the State Council, the highest organ of the central government, was to implement the decisions of the Politburo. At local levels, Party committees were decision-makers; and their corresponding government offices executed their decisions. Second, the Party monopolized power not only through its decision-making but also through its direct control over high officials in the government. Before 1954 China differed from the Soviet Union in that central leaders in China could be either Communists or non-Communists, whereas only Communists could assume high positions in the Soviet Union. This difference largely disappeared as a result of the 1954 NPC elections in China. After the elections, Communists held virtually all the leadership positions in the PRC's central government.

In the midst of the political transition came the PRC's first political purges. Known as the "Gao-Rao affair" after the surnames of two main figures involved, this event revealed the intensity of elite frictions in CCP politics during this period. Gao Gang was one of the most powerful leaders in China. He was the youngest vice president of the PRC, a Politburo member, head of the Central Planning Commission, and the top Party, government, and military official of the Northeast (formerly Manchuria) region. Rao Shushi was director of the CCP Central Committee's organization department, which controlled high-level appointments; a Planning Commission member; and the leading Party and government figure of the East China region. Acting on cues that Mao was not entirely satisfied with Liu Shaoqi (1898–1969), his apparent successor, Gao and Rao colluded to oust Liu and his associates and advance their own careers. As

Gao later admitted, his goal was to replace Liu as Mao's successor as the leader of the country. Their plot, however, backfired when Mao condemned their "factional" activities. Gao commited suicide in August 1954; his main accomplice, Rao Shushi, was stripped of all his official titles and expelled from the Party.

Somewhat interrupted by this unpleasant episode, the Eighth National Congress of the CCP convened in September 1956. Since the convening of the Seventh National Congress 11 years earlier, CCP membership had swelled from only 1.2 million to 10.7 million, and the Party's power was now firmly entrenched. The Eighth National Congress passed a new constitution for the CCP and elected a new leadership, with Mao as chairman; Liu, Zhou Enlai, Zhu De, and Chen Yun as vice chairmen; and Deng Xiaoping as general secretary.

In the economic realm, the CCP decided to accelerate the pace of socialist transformation. The five economic sectors, according to Mao's analysis, had different characters from the perspective of socialism. The state-owned sector was socialist in character, the cooperative sector semi-socialist, and the rest non-socialist. Since the goal of the CCP was to lead China toward socialism—a state of collective prosperity based on social equality—it decided to strengthen the socialist and semi-socialist sectors and phase out the non-socialist sectors.

Although the five-sector economy had originally been projected to last for 10 to 20 years, Mao in 1952 had begun to outline a more rapid transition to socialism. Instead of keeping the five sectors, the CCP decided to phase out private and individual sectors and transform them into cooperative or state-owned sectors. In the rural areas, individual peasants were encouraged to form different types of cooperatives in three stages. At the first stage, they were encouraged to form mutual aid teams, in which six or seven households pooled their labor, tools, and draft animals and helped

During the 1950s, the Chinese government grouped peasant farmers into communes, in which they worked together to grow crops. This process, called collectivization, was based on a Soviet economic model.

one another during the harvest season. At the second stage, mutual aid teams were merged into lower-level agricultural producer cooperatives (APCs), with membership between 30 and 50 households. At this stage, peasants still held title to the land they contributed to the APCs, and they received a dividend according to the size of their land. At the third stage, the lower-level APCs were further merged into the higher-level APCs, which typically consisted of 200 to more than 1,000 households. At this stage, the land had been collectivized, and members of the APCs were no longer entitled to the dividend on the land. Their income depended only on their labor contributions. By the end of 1956, about 90 percent of households in rural China had joined the higher-level APCs. The process of "collectivization" had been completed.

Simultaneously, socialist transformation in industry and commerce had also gone through two stages. At the first stage, private enterprises were encouraged to form joint state-private enterprises; at the second stage, the joint state-private enterprises became state-owned enterprises. In many places the first stage was simply skipped at the urging of local CCP leaders, and private enterprises were transformed into state enterprises in one step.

These changes brought China's economic structure much closer to that of the Soviet Union. The CCP monopolized the economy through state enterprises and the higher-level APCs. In the meantime, China had also adopted the Soviet model in economic planning, which was based on five-year production targets. By the end of 1956 China had fulfilled its first Five-Year Plan (1953–57).

1956年到1967年全国农业发展纲要(草案)

中华人民共和国毛泽东主席在1956年1月25日召集最高国务会议，讨论中共中央提出的1956年到1967年全国农业发展纲要草案，图为毛泽东主席在会上讲话的情形。

(一) 1956年全国基本上完成初级形式的农业合作化

在1955年，已经有60％以上的农户加入农业生产合作社的基础上，要求各省、市，自治区在1956年基本上完成初级形式的农业生产合作化，达到85％左右的农户加入农业生产合作社。

85%

60%

(二) 1958年全国基本上完成高级形式的农业合作化

农业合作基础较好而且工作力量较强的地区，在1957年基本上完成高级形式的农业合作化，其他地区，则要求在1956年，每县办一个至几个较大型(100户以上)的较社，作为榜样，在1958年基本上完成高级形式的农业合作化。

初级社转高级社，应该具备高的条件，以免包办代替，有损社内的领导作用，但是也要转高级社，当革命的领导水平提高，有90％以上的社员增加收入时，可以一个乡一片的办较社，应在合作社较健全的转为高级社，不可就把村村转为高级社的来。

(三) 照顾鳏寡孤独和残废军人

农业生产合作社对于社内缺乏劳动力，生活无依靠的鳏寡孤独的农户和残废军人，应在生产上和生活上加以适当的照顾，做到幼有所养，老有所养，病有所医，使这些人的生活无忧而有靠。

(四) 对地主富农分子及其家庭成员入社的办法

对于过去的地主分子和已经改变成份的富农分子等未入社的问题，在1956年内应当加以解决。解决的办法是：(1) 表现较好的，助于生产的，可以允许他们入社，做为社员，但是无论他们改变成份与否，的身份。(2) 表现一般，不好不坏的，允许他们入社，做为候补社员，暂不改变其成份。表现较差的，由社方实行管制生产，但暂不给予改变成份的制度。(4)过去的地主富农分子，凡属改变已经改变阶级成份但居住农村的，应入社以后的一定时期内，都应加他们在任何事业的职务。(5) 合作社对参加生产的地主富农分子在社内的劳动，应当贯彻同工同酬的原则。(6)地主富农分子，和其是上地改革的情况，他应是青年不是18岁青年在各学校读书的在学学生，如果在上地改革以前，他既非本村农，应在吊富农中那样的地位内，这样人不应当在做地主富农分子看待，凡符合入社们入社，做为社员，并尽量给他们创造入社的条件，分配适当的工作。

(五) 处理农村中反革命分子的办法

对于农村中的反革命分子，应当按照以下的规定加以处理：(1) 进行破坏活动的分子和罪恶历史下的反革命分子，依照法令办法。(2) 凡有一般的罪恶罪行，没有现行破坏而数民愤不大的分子，由乡人民委员会合作社管制生产，劳动改造。(3) 凡有轻微罪行，现在已经停止活动的分子，对没民自居他们何行管制的程度和情况的大小，有的放为社员，(1) 较轻有反革命性的，和力量大，有的放为社员，根据他们入社后的一定时期内的表现，在入社以后的一定时期内，(4)对于受合作社管制生产的反革命分子，合作社应当依照同工同酬的原则，给他们以应有的报酬，(5) 对社会反革命分子的家属，凡属他们没有参加反革命分子的，应当无分别对待，尤其应当允许一起和认真同事，不要歧视他们。

This Chinese poster details the government's plan for the development of agriculture during the period 1956–1967. Mao's ambitious plan for economic growth—known as the Great Leap Forward—was a dismal failure.

The Hundred Flowers and the Great Leap Forward

In his report to the Seventh Congress of the CCP in May 1945, Liu Shaoqi mentioned Mao's name 105 times and introduced Mao Zedong Thought as the guideline for all work of the Party. "Our comrade Mao Zedong," Liu said, "is not only the greatest revolutionary and statesman in the whole history of China, but also the greatest theorist and scientist in the whole history of China." Furthermore, Liu maintained, "Mao Zedong Thought is the only correct guiding thought and the only correct general line of our Party." Under his suggestion, Mao Zedong Thought, the combination of Marxist theory with Chinese practice, was enshrined in the CCP constitution as the guideline for the Party.

Eleven years later, in September 1956, the story was

quite different. In a much longer report to the Eighth Congress, Liu referred to Mao Zedong in only four places and did not mention Mao Zedong Thought at all. The resultant CCP constitution deleted Mao Zedong Thought as the guideline for all work by the Party.

One of the reasons for deleting Mao Zedong Thought from the CCP constitution was external. In February 1956, a few months before the convening of the Eighth Congress of the CCP, the Soviet leader Nikita Khrushchev delivered a speech to the Twentieth Congress of the Soviet Communist Party in which he denounced Stalin (who had died in March 1953). Khrushchev attributed the reign of terror under Stalin to his "cult of personality." Stalin had been worshipped almost as a deity, and he and the Soviet state were seen as virtually one and the same. Those who held opinions different from Stalin's—or whom Stalin merely suspected of disloyalty—were purged (that is, dismissed, imprisoned, or executed).

Mao Zedong meets with Nikita Khrushchev during the Soviet leader's 1958 visit to Beijing. Khrushchev's denunciation of the "cult of personality" in the Soviet Union may have inspired Chinese Communist leaders to try to rein in Mao's power.

Mao and his colleagues learned different lessons from the episode in the Soviet Union. For Liu and others, Khrushchev probably did the right thing in denouncing Stalin and criticizing his personality cult. For Mao, Khrushchev made a mistake not only in his harsh assessment of Stalin but also in indiscriminately attacking the cult of personality.

In order to prevent the kinds of excesses that had taken place during Stalin's rule from happening in China, Liu and others decided to rein in Mao's cult of personality: they would treat him not as some sort of deity but as a fallible human being. The first step in this direction was to remove Mao Zedong Thought from the CCP constitution.

Mao was dismayed that his colleagues were treating him as if he were a deceased Stalin while he was still alive. As Professor Roderick MacFarquhar, a noted China scholar, observed, "For Mao the 8th Congress may have seemed like a litmus paper, revealing his colleagues in their true colors. After leading the revolution successfully for twenty-one years, he may well have been disappointed that a positive attitude towards himself was not more widely in evidence."

The Hundred Flowers and the Anti-Rightist Campaign

A positive attitude toward the leadership role of the CCP was not widely in evidence either, especially among intellectuals. Since 1951 they had been mistreated, humiliated, and even punished in various campaigns. Because of their supposed bourgeois (that is, middle-class and capitalistic) backgrounds, they were put through an extensive period of ideological training, known as "thought reform." During this process, various means were used to get them to acknowledge the "error" of their thinking and to accept the ideology of the CCP. Yet the thought reform of intellectuals was often supervised by CCP cadres with little or no education. In one instance, a Party cadre snatched a letter from a professor's hand while the professor was reading. "I must check what you read," the cadre huffed. The startled professor noted, however, that the cadre was holding the letter upside down!

Chinese intellectuals, as the CCP defined the term, constituted a small percentage of the population. But, as Premier Zhou Enlai explained to a group of political elites in January 1956, they were very important to China's future. Out of 500 million people in China, Zhou said, there were no more than 5 million intellectuals (those who had successfully finished high school); there were only about 100,000 high-level scientists, research workers, and university professors. They were the only pool of knowledge and expertise in China, and they were needed for China's modernization efforts. "Without scientists, without teachers," he continued, "we shall not be able to lift ourselves out of backwardness." Intellectuals, as he defined them, were part of the working class. They should be trusted, supported, and encouraged in their intellectual pursuits. Zhou's speech was the prelude to a brief period of intellectual freedom, known as the Hundred Flowers Movement.

Intellectuals' initial reaction to Zhou's speech was at best guarded; many recalled earlier mistreatment at the hands of the Party. But in April 1956 Mao made a long speech in which he echoed Zhou's call for intellectual freedom. Adopting a suggestion from Guo Moro (1892–1978), a famous scholar, Mao labeled this new direction the Hundred Flowers Movement. That name came from a Chinese idiom dating to around 500 B.C.: "let a hundred flowers bloom, and let a hundred schools of thought contend."

In May, Lu Dingyi, director of the Propaganda Department of the CCP, circulated a version of Mao's speech in all universities in China. What intellectuals really wanted, according to Guo Moro, was an intellectual renaissance—and that seemed to be coming. It appeared that intellectuals would be allowed to hold different opinions from those of the Party, as Mao assured them in a February 1957 speech on the correct handling of "contradictions" among the people. To drive his point home, Mao declared on May 1 that the Hundred Flowers Movement was a political movement in which Party cadres should solicit criticism of their behavior and actions from the intellectuals.

The expected "gentle breeze and mild rain" of comments, suggestions, and remarks, however, quickly turned into a tornado of bitter recrimination, denunciation, and condemnation. Scientists, professors, students, writers, and others spoke up negatively about the leadership of the CCP. They criticized almost everything in China: from the way classes were taught in schools to the cutting down of old trees. Some even attacked political leaders by name. One headline in the *People's Daily*, the mouthpiece of the CCP, ran: "Mao Zedong, Zhou Enlai, it is time for you to step down."

Things were not going the way Mao had expected, and very soon he decided to end the PRC's experiment with freedom of expression. On June 8 the Anti-Rightist Campaign was launched. It appears that Mao originally did not intend to punish too many people. On June 29, 1957, he estimated that there were in the country about 4,000 rightists (broadly, a rightist was someone said to oppose the Communist Party). Ten days later, he doubled that estimate. In September, he further revised the figure, to 150,000. Ultimately, however, the actual number of people who were classified as rightists exceeded 550,000. The consequences of being labeled a rightist were severe: punishment usually included detention—often for lengthy periods—in a "reeducation camp." There the inmate would perform forced labor while undergoing "ideological reform."

The Great Leap Forward and the Great Famine

Around the time the Anti-Rightist Campaign was rooting out real or imagined opponents of socialism, Mao began to chart a new economic course for China. His ambitious plan, designed to help China

This 1957 poster shows views of economic life in China, including images of a manufacturing plant, a map of industrial facilities, and charts showing economic growth. In the early days of the Great Leap Forward, CCP leaders predicted that China would quickly catch up with industrialized nations like Great Britain and the United States.

catch up rapidly with the industrialized nations, would ultimately produce catastrophic results.

In the early years of the People's Republic, Soviet influence was prevalent in all spheres of economic and social life in China. As China's "elder brother," the Soviet Union had been a model not only in economic planning but also in almost everything else. Since the Soviet Union's today was considered China's tomorrow, the Chinese tended to copy what the Soviets did.

Yet the Soviet economic model, as Mao came to know it in 1956, had its own shortcomings. He remarked in an April speech on "Ten Great Relationships" that the Soviet model put undue emphasis on heavy industry and neglected light industry and agriculture. As a result, he explained, those countries that had adopted the model did not have enough goods in the market, their daily necessities were in short supply, and their currencies were unstable. Another problem with the Soviet model, according to Mao, was the concentration of administrative power in the hands of central ministries. This was not good because it shackled the local authorities and denied them the right to independent action. Moreover, as relations between China and the Soviet Union deteriorated, it would be impossible for China to continue to expect the same support and assistance from the Soviet Union as before.

China, as Mao envisioned, would avoid all these problems. It would develop all economic sectors simultaneously. China would combine centralization of ministerial control with decentralization of local initiatives. China would also be prepared for "self-reliance" in economic construction. This rational, balanced approach was later adopted by the Eighth Congress and was written into the Second Five-Year Plan (1958–1962).

But Mao soon abandoned this approach after his visit to Moscow in November 1957. The Soviet Union had just successfully launched the first artificial earth satellite, *Sputnik*, on October 4, 1957. The Soviet Union, as Khrushchev announced, was planning to catch up with the United States in the output of major industrial products, such as iron ore, iron, steel, coal, oil, and electricity, in 15 years. Mao was greatly impressed by the Soviet achievements and by the Soviet plans. Meanwhile, he was also under tremendous pressure to improve China's economy much faster than had been planned. If the Soviet Union could catch up with the United States, he wondered, why couldn't China catch up with Great Britain?

Partly as a race between China and the Soviet Union (or more precisely, a race between Mao and Khrushchev), a new campaign, the Great Leap Forward (GLF), was launched in China. Although the general line of the GLF was said to be "going all out and aiming high to achieve greater, faster, better, and more economical (results) in socialist construction," speed and quantity would be the key features of the GLF. In November 1957, Mao proposed for China to catch up with Britain in steel production in 15 years. In April 1958, Liu Shaoqi indicated that China would probably catch up with Britain in 10 years. One month later, at the Second Meeting of the Eighth National Congress of the CCP, after Mao further revised the estimate to 7 years, ministerial leaders of metallurgy reported that China could actually surpass Britain in 5 years and catch up with the United States in 15 years.

As cadres at all levels—from central ministries through provinces, prefectures, municipalities, and counties, all the way to villages—were ratcheting up their targets in steel production, actual production was far from reaching these ambitious goals. On June 19, 1958, after several revisions, Mao finally set the target in steel production for 1958 at 10.7 million tons, twice as much as had been produced in 1957. By the end of August, when this number was announced, however, China had produced only 4.5 million tons. With just four months left in the year, China was still 6.2 million tons short of the goal. In other words, China had fulfilled one-third of the plan within two-thirds of the year, but now it had to complete two-thirds of the plan within one-third of the year.

Under Mao's direction, all levels of Chinese society were mobilized to meet the steel production goals. People from all walks of life and all ages—workers, peasants, soldiers, store clerks, and college, middle school, and elementary school students and their professors and teachers—participated. Millions of backyard furnaces were built, and anything containing iron or steel—furniture, bicycles, clothes hangers, pots and pans—was collected and melted down in the furnaces. On December 19, it was declared that the target had been met; by the end of 1958, Chinese steel production for the year was reported at 11.08 million tons. The apparent miracle, however, was illusory. Only 8 million tons of the steel China produced was actually usable. Plus, finished goods had been melted down for the production of raw materials—a highly irrational endeavor. Ultimately, an enormous amount of effort had been expended for no real benefit.

In the meantime, the Great Leap Forward was transforming the countryside. In 1958 the government mandated the creation of "people's communes," more than 20,000 of which were established. Each commune controlled its own means of production, in keeping with Communist theory, and was managed by Party

Welders at a steel factory in China, circa 1950.

members (who usually came from outside the community). Whereas farmers in the agricultural collectives had been able to profit personally from their labor (this had been referred to as "self-exploitation"), commune residents all received the same remuneration. This removed a major incentive to work hard and was one reason that agricultural production fell. Other reasons for declining production were confusion over new roles and responsibilities and the ineptitude of some commune managers.

Land was also taken out of agricultural use for the construction of factories, as Mao had wanted to promote China's light-manufacturing

'BY GOVERNMENT DEGREE EVERY MEMBER OF THE COMMUNE IS ENTITLED TO A PRIVATE LOT'

In 1961, after a period of prolonged bad weather and the ill-advised policies of the Great Leap Forward, China experienced a severe famine. The government was forced to relax centralized control of the agricultural communes and even to give farmers the right to farm their own plots. In this political cartoon from 1961, U.S. artist Edmund S. Valtman suggests that the only plots many Chinese will receive will be their own graves.

sector. Unfortunately, many of the former farmers who worked in these factories had little idea how to use the machinery efficiently.

Compounding these problems was the fact that commune managers answered to the central government and thus had an incentive to inflate production figures in order to advance their own careers. Beginning in 1958, record crop yields were reported, with one producer seemingly outdoing the next in rapid succession. The problem was that the communes had to give a portion of their surplus harvests to the government. Thus, when a manager reported an exaggerated yield, the government took more of the actual crops, leaving the people on the commune with less.

As the GLF continued and peasants were forced to surrender grains from imaginary surpluses, they were left with nothing for themselves. In Henan Province, for instance, the actual production of grain for 1959 was only about 1.05 million tons, but provincial leaders insisted that 2.25 million tons had been produced and asked peasants to meet the state quota based on this fictitious figure. Local cadres used physical violence against peasants who did not (or in most cases could not) meet their demands. In some places people resorted to eating tree bark to survive.

In the end, the Great Leap Forward, in combination with a period of bad weather, produced a famine of unprecedented proportions. Between 1959 and 1962, at least 14 million Chinese people (and perhaps 30 million or more) starved to death.

Scene from the Cultural Revolution: Carrying a large portrait of Chairman Mao, young Red Guards chant and march through the streets, 1968. The decade-long Cultural Revolution claimed millions of victims and turned Chinese society upside down.

The Cultural Revolution

In the wake of the economic chaos and devastating famine brought about by the Great Leap Forward, Mao Zedong largely withdrew from public view. With the temporary decline of his political influence, several officials took steps to spur economic recovery and alleviate the plight of China's peasants. Chief among them were Liu Shaoqi, China's president and Mao's apparent successor as head of the Chinese Communist Party, and Deng Xiaoping, the CCP's general secretary. Liu and Deng allowed peasants to keep private plots for their families, to engage in sideline production, and to sell their agricultural products in rural trade fairs. Liu and others also endorsed the "household responsibility system" for production in rural areas, by which individual households, rather than APCs or people's communes, were to assume responsibility for production.

Liu, Deng, and their allies may have viewed these measures as sensible, pragmatic steps to help put China on the road to economic recovery, but Mao Zedong saw in them something far different: signs that capitalism was reemerging. Since 1956, when Khrushchev had denounced Stalin and begun to change his policies in the Soviet Union, Mao had been concerned about such "revisionism" in China. The CCP chairman had feared that his successors might revise his socialist policies after his death, and now it seemed that Liu and Deng were attempting to do that even while he was still alive. Mao was determined to eliminate his revisionist rivals; weed out "bourgeois" influences, which he thought had crept into the CCP and Chinese society; and reawaken revolutionary fervor.

Literary Controversy

Mao's attack on revisionism grew out of a controversy in the cultural sphere. On November 10, 1965, the *Wenhui Daily* published an article, "On the New Historical Play *Dismissal of Hai Rui from Office*," written by the literary critic Yao Wenyuan (b. 1931). The title character of the play, a civil servant during the Ming period (1368–1644), was wrongfully dismissed from office and imprisoned because he told the truth to the emperor. In his article, Yao criticized the author of the play, Wu Han (1909–1969), for perspectives that were politically mistaken—specifically, for denying Chairman Mao's fundamental premise of class struggle by attributing to the historical Hai Rui heroic deeds on behalf of the peasants.

But for Mao, that was not the only troubling aspect of Wu's play. Mao became convinced that *Dismissal of Hai Rui from Office* was attempting to draw analogies between the treatment of the upright Ming dynasty official and the treatment of a recently purged CCP member, Peng Dehuai. In 1959, at the Lushan Conference, Peng, China's defense minister, had been mildly critical of Mao's Great Leap Forward. He was soon denounced as the leader of an anti-

CCP clique and dismissed from office. In Mao's view, playwright Wu Han was linking Hai Rui's dismissal for telling the truth to a Ming emperor with Peng Dehuai's dismissal for telling the truth about the Great Leap Forward.

Mao asked Peng Zhen, a Politburo member in charge of the Five-Man Group—which had been established in 1964 to deal with matters of revolution in culture—to review the case. Peng decided that Wu's play and Yao's article belonged to academic, rather than political, debates; that there was no connection between Wu and Peng Dehuai; and that there was no link between Wu's play and the Lushan Conference. With the endorsement of three other members of the Five-Man Group, Peng then submitted a report in February 1966 to Mao. Not satisfied with Peng's report, Mao decided in April to dissolve the Five-Man Group. At an enlarged meeting of the Politburo in May, Peng Zhen and a number of others were dismissed; the Five-Man Group was replaced by the new Cultural Revolution Group, which included Mao's wife, Jiang Qing (1914–1991); and the May 16 Circular was issued. That document urged CCP loyalists to "hold high the great banner of the proletarian cultural revolution, thoroughly expose the reactionary bourgeois stand of those so-called 'academic authorities' who oppose the Party and socialism, thoroughly criticize and repudiate the reactionary bourgeois ideas in the sphere of academic work, education, journalism, literature and art and publishing, and seize the leadership in these cultural spheres." The Great Proletarian Cultural Revolution—the Cultural Revolution for short—had officially begun.

"Two-Line Struggle" Between Mao and Liu

The May 16 Circular asserted that representatives of the bourgeoisie who had sneaked into the Chinese Communist Party, the government, the military, and all cultural circles were poised to grab power when the time was ripe. But in particular the circular warned that, while some of these revisionists had been exposed, others were "still sleeping by our side"—being trained as successors to Mao—just as Khrushchev had waited for his opportunity in the Soviet Union.

For Mao, the Khrushchev in China who was still sleeping by his side was Liu Shaoqi. It was Liu who deleted Mao Zedong Thought from the CCP constitution in 1956; it was Liu who took his post as the head of state in 1959; it was Liu who indirectly blamed him for the failure of the Great Leap Forward at the Seven Thousand Cadre Conference in 1962, and it was Liu who supported the household responsibility system that same year. Whatever else the Cultural Revolution represented, in the view of some historians it was first and foremost a play by Mao to remove Liu (and like-minded allies) from power.

The seeds of Liu's downfall were sown through a big-character poster (a large-format poster hung in a public place, generally as a means of political communication or protest) by Nie Yuanzi (b. 1921). On May 25, 1966, Nie—a lecturer from Beijing University (Beida)—along with six other faculty members from the Department of Philosophy, posted the poster, which attacked the Party secretary of Beida. Nie had been encouraged by the wife of Kang Sheng (1898–1975), the adviser of the Cultural Revolution Group. Kang's intention seems to have been to fan the flames of controversy and draw in high-level officials. Liu's immediate reaction was to put out the fire: he sent a work team (a task force group) to Beida to calm the situation. Mao's response was to have Nie's poster published, which signaled people at other universities and colleges that they could attack their leaders as well. Yet at the same time, Mao gave his blessing as Liu, Zhou Enlai, and Deng Xiaoping sent work teams to colleges and middle schools. In July, however, Mao accused Liu and Deng of suppressing the student movement and urged them to recall the work teams.

"Those representatives of the bourgeoisie who have sneaked into the party, the government, the army, and various cultural circles are a bunch of counter-revolutionary revisionists. Once conditions are ripe, they will seize political power and turn the dictatorship of the proletariat into a dictatorship of the bourgeoisie. Some of them we have already seen through, others we have not. Some are still trusted by us and are being trained as our successors. . . . Party committees at all levels must pay full attention to this matter."

—Excerpt from the
May 16 Circular

On July 29, Liu was forced into self-criticism at a meeting in the Great Hall of the People. He confessed that he was confused about how to bring about the Cultural Revolution. "You ask us how we should bring about this revolution," he said. "I honestly tell you that I don't know. Our comrades in the Central Committee of our Party and the members of the work teams don't know either." It was true, for what Liu was really being asked to do was conduct a revolution against himself.

Following a big-character poster from Mao during the Eleventh Plenum of the Eighth Central Committee in August 1966, Liu was

Chinese students read from the Little Red Book in front of a poster of Mao.

demoted from No. 2 in the Party to No. 8. At the enlarged Twelfth Plenum of the Eighth Central Committee in October 1968, Liu was dismissed from all his government and Party positions and expelled from the CCP "once and for all." Described as a "renegade, traitor, and scab hiding in the Party" and as a "lackey of imperialism, modern revisionism, and Guomindang reactionaries," he was accused of having "committed innumerable counter-revolutionary crimes." One year later, in November 1969, Liu died in captivity in Kaifeng, Henan.

Deng Xiaoping, branded the "number two capitalist roader," fared slightly better. He was stripped of his Party and government posts and banished to a tractor-repair factory.

The Red Guards and Revolutionary Rebels

Mao's Cultural Revolution drew its foot soldiers mostly from the ranks of the young. After the release of the May 16 Circular, a group of Beijing high school students calling themselves the "Red Guards of Mao's Thought" had formed to defend the Party chairman "to the death" if necessary. With Mao's encouragement, other high school and university students formed units of what came to be called simply the Red Guards. Spouting excerpts from *Quotations from Chairman Mao*—the famous Little Red Book—these young militants terrorized "hidden enemies" of China's revolution, which turned out to include a significant portion of the country's inhabitants. Students in the Red Guards denounced and removed their teachers and school administrators, in many cases forcing the closure of entire schools; some teachers were beaten to death for their supposed bourgeois sympathies or other ideological transgressions. In response to Mao's call for rebellion against "capitalist roaders" in power at all levels, factory workers also formed their own organizations of "Revolutionary Rebels" and denounced their managers. Professionals and other "intellectuals" were condemned for putting "technical expertise" before "correct political thinking." Party and government leaders were accused of taking the capitalist road and were removed from office en masse.

The Cultural Revolution produced enormous disruption in Chinese society. Red Guards roamed freely throughout the country, exposing the "mistakes" of terror-stricken citizens; often bands of young militants stormed into random homes to beat the occupants and destroy their possessions. Revolutionary Rebel groups interrupted production and challenged Party and government authorities. In early 1967 Red Guards groups ousted municipal authorities in Shanghai and seized power in that city. Similar battles played out in other locales, and different Red Guards or Revolutionary Rebel factions sometimes fought one another for control. In Wuhan in 1968, two Revolutionary Rebel coalitions (one of which was supported by local People's Liberation Army troops) clashed, paralyzing the local Party and government and shutting down factories. Ultimately the People's Liberation Army, under the command of Lin Biao (1907–1971), would be called on to restore order in China.

In late 1968, in keeping with Mao's instructions, about 2 million students were sent to the countryside to be "reeducated" by the peasants (eventually that number would reach 12 million). While the Cultural Revolution would sputter along for another eight years, in the process perpetuating social chaos, dividing countless families, and producing hundreds of thousands of additional victims, Mao had by this time already achieved what in retrospect appears to have been his central goal: ousting Liu Shaoqi and purging the CCP of the "capitalist roaders" who he felt had infiltrated the ranks of the Party's leadership.

Rise and Fall of Lin Biao

The biggest beneficiary of the downfall of Liu Shaoqi and Deng Xiaoping—and before them, of Peng Dehuai—was Lin Biao. Lin—who had won a reputation as a brilliant Red Army commander during China's civil war—replaced Peng as minister of defense in 1959 and replaced Liu as No. 2 person in the Party (vice chairman of the CCP) in 1966. His secret of success was promoting Mao's personality cult. Whereas Liu, at the Seven Thousand Cadre Conference

The Little Red Book

During the Cultural Revolution, the *Quotations from Chairman Mao* was as indispensable to a member of the Red Guards as a rifle is to an infantry soldier. The Little Red Book, as it was popularly known, offered authoritative guidance on such topics as "The Correct Handling of Contradictions Among the People," "Correcting Mistaken Ideas," and "Criticism and Self-Criticism," and young Red Guards students used it to expose the "errors" of countless teachers, intellectuals, parents, and other supposed enemies of the revolution.

The Little Red Book was the brainchild of Lin Biao, who compiled the handbook of quotations from Mao and saw that copies were distributed throughout China. Lin also wrote the book's preface, in which he urged, "Study Chairman Mao's writings, follow his teachings and act according to his instructions."

Lin—often referred to in the Chinese press as Mao's "best student"—was later accused of plotting to assassinate the chairman.

in January 1962, had cast some of the blame for the failures of the Great Leap Forward and the resulting famine upon Mao, Lin expressed a completely different view. "The difficulties are caused by the fact that we have not followed Chairman Mao's instructions," he argued. "If we had, the problems would be less, and the obstacles smaller." He then praised Mao Zedong Thought and Mao effusively. "The correct ideology is . . . Mao Zedong Thought," Lin said. "Chairman Mao has many merits. According to my long-term personal observation, Chairman Mao's greatest asset is his grasp of reality. He has stuck to and never deviated from reality. When we

In this May 1967 photo Lin Biao (left) holds a copy of the Little Red Book; behind him are Zhou Enlai (wearing dark jacket) and Chen Boda (wearing glasses and cap). Although Lin Biao maneuvered into a position as Mao's designated successor in 1969, he soon lost favor with the chairman. After his supporter Chen Boda was purged in 1970, Lin Biao is said to have planned a coup, which failed in September 1971; Lin was apparently killed in a plane crash while attempting to flee the country.

followed Chairman Mao's thought, we did well; when we didn't, something went wrong. This is what history tells us."

Thus were planted the seeds for the decline of Liu and the rise of Lin. At the Ninth National Congress of the CCP in April 1969, Mao and Lin both got what they wanted: Mao Zedong Thought was restored in the CCP constitution as the guideline for the Party, and Lin was designated as "Comrade Mao Zedong's close comrade-in-arms and successor."

He would not enjoy that honored status for very long: at the Lushan Conference the following year, it was evident that Lin was losing—or perhaps had already lost—favor with Mao. The chairman harshly criticized Chen Boda, one of Lin's followers, and Chen was soon purged. Mao is said to have been irritated by Lin's insistence on inscrting into the new state constitution the adverbs "with genius, creatively, and comprehensively" in a description of the chairman's contributions to Marxism, and by Lin's insistence that the People's Republic of China have the post of head of state. Mao had previously rejected both the language describing his contributions to Marxism and the creation of the head of state position. Under the surface of these seemingly trivial differences lay Mao's growing uneasiness over the political ambitions of his "best student." Mao was concerned about Lin's domination of the military, and about the military's control in civil affairs. By late summer of 1971 Mao had publicly alluded to Lin's inappropriate ambitions, a clear sign that his days in the Party were numbered.

Recognizing that Lin had lost the chairman's confidence and that he might be removed from power at any moment, Lin's son, Lin Liguo, an air force officer, plotted to kill Mao and assembled a contingent of supporters to carry out the plot. After the assassination attempt failed, Lin, along with his wife, Lin Liguo, and several others, tried to flee China in the early morning of September 13, 1971, aboard a plane bound for the Soviet Union, but their plane crashed near Undur Khan in Mongolia, killing all nine on board. Following Lin's demise, many top commanders in the armed forces were either purged or rotated among different regions.

Sino-U.S. Rapprochement

Lin's death, according to a Central Committee circular, was well deserved for his traitorous activities: he betrayed his motherland for the Soviet Union, the circular claimed. Sino-Soviet relations had deteriorated throughout the 1960s. In July 1960, when China was in desperate straits because of the Great Leap Forward–triggered economic disruptions and famine, the Soviet Union recalled its expert advisers in China and unilaterally canceled all of its contracts with the People's Republic. By the end of the decade, the growing animosity between the two Communist nations would erupt in fighting along their border. In March 1969, Soviet and Chinese troops engaged in a series of clashes over Zhenbao (Damansky) Island in the Ussuri River. In the eyes of Mao and Zhou Enlai, the Soviet Union had become their country's most dangerous enemy.

The rift with the Soviet Union partly explains China's openness to better relations with the United States. In December 1969, the U.S. ambassador to Poland indicated that he was authorized by Washington to resume contacts with the Chinese embassy in Poland. In April 1971, the Chinese Ping-Pong team at the Nagoya World Championships in Japan invited the U.S. team to visit China. Following this opening, which would be dubbed "Ping-Pong diplomacy," Dr. Henry Kissinger, President Richard Nixon's assistant for national security affairs and special envoy, arrived in Beijing on July 9, 1971, for a secret visit. On October 25, the United Nations voted to expel Taiwan and admit the People's Republic of China.

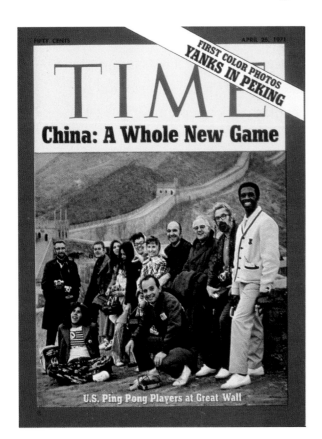

The cover of *Time* magazine from April 26, 1971, features a photo of the U.S. table tennis team posing on the Great Wall. The team's invitation to play in China was one of the first steps toward better U.S.-Chinese relations.

President Richard M. Nixon meets with Mao Zedong on February 29, 1972.

Early the following year, President Nixon visited China. At noon on February 21, 1972, Nixon disembarked from his plane and extended his hand to Premier Zhou Enlai. Zhou took Nixon's hand and told him, "You have extended your hand over the largest ocean of the world and over twenty-five years." The historic handshake shook the world and dramatically altered the course of superpower relations. Nixon's visit began a process of rapprochement—the establishment of cordial relations—between China and the United States (although the two countries would not establish full diplomatic relations with each other until January 1, 1979).

Return of Deng Xiaoping

Upon hearing the news of Lin Biao's death, Deng Xiaoping, former CCP general secretary and China's "number two capitalist roader," wrote a letter to Chairman Mao in November 1971. Deng followed up with another letter to Mao in August 1972. In these letters, Deng admitted his past errors, criticized Lin, and asked to work once more for the Party and the people. Mao's response was positive. He remarked in January 1972 that Deng's case was one of "the contradictions among the people" and observed in late 1972 that Deng was different from Liu Shaoqi. Deng and his family were allowed to return to Beijing from Jiangxi in February 1973. In April, after a formal resolution the previous month, Deng made his first public appearance since 1966, as vice premier.

Initially, no serious conflicts were apparent between Deng and Mao's wife, Jiang Qing, and her associates (later known as the Gang of Four). In fact, it was Jiang who had delivered Deng's second letter to Mao in August 1972. Deng did not seem to pose any threat to her power, for he failed to enter the Politburo at the First Plenum of the Tenth Central Committee in August 1973. In the meantime, the Gang of Four (Jiang Qing, Zhang Chunqiao, Yao Wenyuan, and Wang Hongwen) were all Politburo members; two of them, Zhang and Wang, were standing members of the Politburo; and one of them, Wang, was a vice chairman of the Party. As Deng's power grew, however, he came into direct clashes with the Gang of Four. Deng made it into the Politburo in December 1973 under Mao's recommendation, and in January 1975 he was made a standing member of the Politburo as well as a vice chairman of the Party under Zhou's recommendation. Moreover, Deng was also first vice premier, vice chairman of the Central Military Commission (CMC), and chief of staff of the People's Liberation Army.

Following the Fourth National People's Congress of January 1975, Deng took a series of measures to restore production and rectify the problems created by the Cultural Revolution. The Gang of Four accused Deng of restoring capitalism in China. Appealing to Mao's attachment to the Cultural Revolution, they launched a campaign to "repulse the right deviationist wind" in November 1975 and had Deng removed from office after the death of Zhou Enlai on January 8, 1976.

Hua Guofeng and the Fall of the Gang of Four

Under the influence of his nephew, Mao Yuanxin (b. 1941), Mao was convinced that Deng was changing the course of his Cultural Revolution. Following the death of Premier Zhou, Mao chose Hua Guofeng (b. 1920) as acting premier. Hua had been vice premier, minister of public security, and Party secretary of Hunan Province.

Within a few months, however, widespread public dissatisfaction with the Cultural Revolution, and with Jiang Qing, became apparent in what came to be called the April Fifth Movement. A mass display of affection for the deceased Zhou—which also constituted implicit criticism of Jiang and support for Deng—turned violent in Tiananmen Square on April 5. The government moved quickly to silence the dissenters, and on April 7 Mao removed Deng from office and appointed Hua as premier and first vice chairman of the Party.

Mao's wife, Jiang Qing (1914–1991), was a leader of the Cultural Revolution and a member of China's Politburo. As one of the notorious Gang of Four, she held a great deal of power in the country.

The political landscape of China would change dramatically before the end of the year, however. Mao, who had led the People's Republic of China since its founding in 1949, passed away at 12:10 A.M. on September 9, 1976. He was 83.

Although Hua was Mao's choice, Jiang Qing was also interested in succeeding her husband as the head of the Party. At a Politburo meeting on September 29, she asked, "Now that Chairman Mao has passed away, what should we do about the leadership of the Party?" Her associates, Wang Hongwen and Zhang Chunqiao, then followed with a request to find an appropriate position for Jiang. Ye Jianying (1897–1986), vice chairman of the Party and vice chairman of the Central Military Commission, retorted that since

After Mao's death Hua Guofeng, shown here waving at a November 1976 rally in Tiananmen Square, became China's premier. He quickly arrested the Gang of Four, placing them on trial for crimes against the state and ending the Cultural Revolution.

Jiang already had membership in the Politburo—which was an important position by itself—it was not necessary to find her another position.

It appeared that a clash between the Gang of Four and Hua and Ye was inevitable. Both sides were mobilized for a showdown. On October 2, Mao Yuanxin reportedly ordered an armored division into Beijing. But on October 6, Hua and Ye preempted any move by their rivals, as the Gang of Four and Mao Yuanxin were all arrested. After 10 years, the Cultural Revolution was finally over. During that chaotic decade at least half a million lives had been lost to violence; numerous families had been shattered; schools and colleges had been closed for an extended period, creating a "lost generation" of Chinese youth; almost all Party and government officials had been humiliated or even tortured; and a great many officials had been removed from their posts.

Chinese leader Deng Xiaoping and U.S. president Jimmy Carter sign diplomatic agreements between their respective countries, January 31, 1979.

9

Reform and Conflict

After the arrest of the Gang of Four, Hua became the most powerful man in China. He was premier, chairman of the Party, and chairman of the Central Military Commission. In one person, he combined the posts of both Mao and Zhou. As Mao's successor, he continued to carry out Mao's policies. His formula for China was summed up as "two whatevers": "whatever policy Chairman Mao decided upon, we shall resolutely defend; whatever directives Chairman Mao issued, we shall steadfastly obey."

By July 1977, however, Deng Xiaoping had worked his way back onto the political stage, and as his influence increased, Hua's power slipped. While Hua retained his official titles, in a little more than a year Deng had consolidated actual power in his own hands. It was Deng who initiated economic reforms at the Third Plenum of the Eleventh Central Committee in December 1978. It was Deng who visited Japan in late 1978 and the United States in early 1979 on behalf of the Chinese government. It was also Deng who removed Hua's supporters (known as "the little gang of four") for their advocacy of "whateverism." When Wang Dongxing, Mao's former guard and vice chairman of the Party, questioned the reversal of the official verdict on Liu Shaoqi and asked, "Who would take the responsibility if there are negative repercussions?" Deng Xiaoping stood up and said, "Me!"

Economic Reforms and Opening to the Outside World

One of the reasons that Deng Xiaoping had been purged in 1966 was his so-called cat theory, which promoted pragmatism over ideological inflexibility in economic matters. Upon learning that some villages had recovered from the consequences of the Great Leap Forward because of a household responsibility system, Deng uttered a folk rhyme in support of that approach: "Black cat, white cat, it is a good cat as long as it catches mice." However, he was later criticized by Mao for taking the capitalist road.

In 1978 Anhui Province, where the household responsibility system had originated in 1960, suffered such a serious drought that many peasants had to abandon their homes to beg elsewhere. But Xiaogang, one of the poorest villages in the province, decided to give the household responsibility system a try. One night in December, 20 households gathered for a secret meeting. Since the system was explicitly forbidden in the central policy, they were taking a great risk. Their gamble paid off. By the end of 1979, their agricultural production quadrupled. For the first time since 1956, the village had surplus grains. News of their success soon spread to neighboring villages, which also adopted the household responsibility system. Wan Li (b. 1916), Party secretary of the province, was an enthusiastic supporter of the system, and he received

Taiwanese factory workers prepare bicycle parts for export. The economic success of Taiwan and Hong Kong, and of other Asian countries like South Korea, Singapore, and Japan, encouraged Deng Xiaoping to initiate market-based economic reforms in China.

Deng's blessing. In February 1980, Wan was transferred to Beijing as vice premier in charge of agriculture. The household responsibility system soon spread to the whole country. The peasants, who had suffered the most during the Great Leap Forward, were the first to benefit from economic reforms.

In 1979 Deng also decided to open up China to the outside world for trade and investment. Four areas in the provinces of Guangdong and Fujian were selected for establishing special economic zones. These four areas were chosen for their proximity to external financial resources and accessibility: Shenzhen is just north of Hong Kong; Zhuhai is adjacent to Macao; and Shantou and Xiamen are opposite Taiwan. China's foreign trade increased rapidly, from $9.7 billion in 1978 to $26.1 billion in 1984. Foreign investment in China also grew, from almost nothing in 1978 to $1.3 billion in 1984. In 1984 China opened up 14 more coastal cities— many of them the ports that China had been forced to open to foreigners more than a century earlier.

"One Country, Two Systems"

Deng also crafted policies designed to resolve territorial issues important to China—specifically, the reunification of Taiwan with Mainland China and the return of Hong Kong and Macao. Taiwan had been separated from the mainland since 1949, when Jiang Jieshi and his supporters retreated to the island. Under the leadership of the GMD, Taiwan experienced impressive economic growth, achieving a standard of living for its people that far outstripped the standard of living in the People's Republic. Deng proposed a principle of "one country, two systems" as the basis for Taiwanese reunification with the mainland. According to this principle, Taiwan would be allowed to retain its social and economic systems after reunification, and two different systems (socialism and capitalism) would coexist within the PRC.

To maintain stability and prosperity in Hong Kong and Macao, Deng applied the same principle to these two areas as well. He negotiated the return of Hong Kong with Margaret Thatcher, Britain's prime minister, between 1982 and 1984, and reached an agreement with the Portuguese on the return of Macao in 1987. Under the principle of "one country, two systems," Hong Kong and Macao would become special administrative regions under their respective basic laws in accordance with the Constitution of the People's Republic of China. Deng promised that the status of these two regions under the principle of "one country, two systems" would be maintained for at least 50 years after their return.

British prime minister Margaret Thatcher visits Hong Kong, December 1984. After several years of negotiations in the early 1980s, Great Britain agreed to hand over control of Hong Kong to China in 1997.

Political Succession

Although he was unquestionably China's actual leader, Deng thrice refused to formally assume the highest position as chairman of the CCP Central Committee. As a farsighted statesman, he was thinking of abolishing the lifelong tenure of political leaders in China and of establishing an institutionalized system of political transition. He selected Hu Yaobang (1915–1989), a veteran of the

Deng Xiaoping (left) and Hu Yaobang acknowledge the crowd at a 1981 event in Beijing. Hu was appointed to replace Hua Guofeng as chairman of the Chinese Communist Party in 1980.

Long March and a man 19 years his junior, as general secretary of the CCP in February 1980 and used Hu to replace Hua Guofeng as chairman of the CCP in June of the following year. He also promoted Zhao Ziyang (b. 1919), former Party secretary of Sichuan, to the post of premier in September 1980; that shake-up also came at the expense of Hua.

In order to rejuvenate the Party's leadership, Deng made efforts to set up a semi-retirement system for high-ranking officials. Historically, political leaders in the PRC would not exit from public life until they were either dead or dismissed from office for political reasons. As a third alternative, Deng created the Central Advisory Commission (CAC) as a way station en route to full retirement for senior Party leaders with more than 40 years of service to the revolution. CAC members would be entitled to retain their full salaries, ranks, and perks, and they would continue to be consulted regularly by Party leaders on matters of importance. But they would cease serving on the Party's regular decision-making bodies, thus making room for younger, more educated, and more technically proficient cadres in bodies such as the Politburo and Central Committee.

The Politics and Pitfalls of Reform

As Deng Xiaoping saw it, the Cultural Revolution had been a catastrophe in which the Chinese people lost their dignity, their assets, and, in many cases, their lives. Furthermore, China's chances to develop economically had been squandered. Deng believed that in order for his country to move forward with the Four Modernizations—of agriculture, industry, defense, and science and technology—China had to avoid a repetition of the Cultural Revolution at all costs. Political stability, he believed, is a precondition for economic growth, and anything that compromised China's political stability would upset its economic development. For this reason, he suppressed the Democracy Wall (a stretch of wall along Xidan Avenue west of Tiananmen Square in Beijing, where big-character posters were posted in support of "the fifth modernization," democracy); introduced the "four cardinal principles" (adherence to the socialist road, the people's democratic dictatorship, Communist Party leadership, and Marxism-Leninism–Mao Zedong Thought); and deleted from the state constitution the right to engage in great debate and to put up big-character posters.

On the question of Mao, Deng was forthright about the chairman's errors, especially during the Cultural Revolution, and demystified his godlike image. But, in contrast to Khrushchev's treatment of Stalin's legacy in the Soviet Union, Deng did not completely denounce Mao and did not abandon Mao Zedong Thought. Through the "Resolution on certain questions in the history of our Party since the founding of the PRC," adopted in July 1981 by the Sixth Plenum of the 11th Central Committee, Deng affirmed the historical role of

Mao, praised Mao's achievements, and upheld Mao Zedong Thought while blaming Mao for the losses and setbacks the country had suffered during the Cultural Revolution. Although it was true that Mao had made "gross mistakes" during the Cultural Revolution, as the resolution assessed him, "if we judge his activities as a whole, his contributions to the Chinese revolution far outweigh his mistakes."

Clearly, Deng's policy in the political sphere was the opposite of his policy in the economic sphere. While he was letting go (called *fang* in Chinese) in economic activities, he was also tightening up (*shou*) in political debates. When a group of Party theoreticians revealed the undemocratic nature of the political system in China and thus indirectly questioned the political legitimacy of the CCP in a veiled debate on "socialist humanism," Deng labeled the phenomenon "spiritual pollution" and called for a vigorous ideological struggle against it. But when the anti-spiritual-pollution campaign began to disrupt his reform and open-door policies, Deng intervened to bring it to a halt.

Yet social tensions became more acute when urban reforms began in 1984. On the one hand, some city dwellers were worse off as a result of the reforms. Because of the removal of price controls on daily necessities such as foods, the cost of living for urban residents rose. As state enterprises were encouraged to smash the "iron rice bowl" (guaranteed lifetime employment, with wages unrelated to job performance) and the "big common pot" (the idea that everyone should share equally in prosperity or poverty), industrial workers were also faced with the prospect of losing their jobs. On the other hand, some urbanites were better off as a result of the reforms. As individual businesses were encouraged to develop, many private entrepreneurs grew prosperous. Children of high-level cadres (known as "princelings") had also thrived because of their family connections. In a widely publicized case, military cadres and their offspring in the duty-free port of Hainan had floated hard-currency bank loans and credits in the amount of $1.25 billion to import 89,000 Toyota automobiles, 2.9 million television sets, 252,000 videocassette recorders, and 122,000 motorcycles for resale on the domestic market at a high profit.

College students grew restive during the mid-1980s. Some were reacting to what they perceived as social injustices. Many others were inspired by a handful of dissidents who had begun openly criticizing the Party and its policies. The most prominent of these dissidents was Fang Lizhi (b. 1936), an internationally known astrophysicist at the Chinese University of Science and Technology (CUST) in Hefei, Anhui Province. Fang called for democracy and intellectual freedom, criticized the abuses and corruption of Party members, and even went so far as to suggest, in a November 1986 speech to students at Tongji University, that "the socialist movement from Marx and Lenin to Stalin and Mao Zedong has been a failure. . . . Clearing our minds of all Marxist dogma is the first step [to reform and modernization]." On December 5, 1986, several hundred students at CUST protested their exclusion both from the process of selecting the head of their local student union and from nominating candidates for the provincial People's Congress. The student demonstrations soon spread to Shanghai, Beijing, Wuhan, Nanjing, Tianjin, Hangzhou, and Shenzhen.

Putting the blame squarely on Hu Yaobang for being soft on student demonstrators, several conservative leaders, including some members of the Central Advisory Commission, persuaded Deng Xiaoping to dismiss Hu. On January 16, 1987, at an enlarged meeting of the Politburo that was also attended by 17 leading members of the CAC, Hu "resigned" as general secretary of the CCP. A campaign against "bourgeois liberalism," targeting intellectuals who had advocated "total Westernization," soon ensued.

At the Thirteenth Party Congress of October to November 1987, where he was elected to succeed Hu as general secretary of the CCP, Zhao Ziyang articulated a reform blueprint for China. According to Zhao's political report, China was at the primary stage of socialism, and the fundamental Party line at this stage was "one center and two basic points." Economic development was to be considered the "central task" of the present stage, to be pursued by grasping simultaneously two "basic points": adherence to the four cardinal principles and persistence in the policy of reform and opening up to the outside world. More specifically, Zhao advocated the creation of private markets for essential factors such as funds, labor services, technology, information, and real estate; he also proposed to conduct limited political reform.

By the end of 1987, however, inflation began to erode consumers' confidence in the Chinese economy. As enterprises vied with one another for granting wage and bonus increases to workers, the money supply substantially increased. As consumer demand rose, output and prices also soared for certain luxury goods, such as automatic washing machines, color TVs, stereo sets, and refrigerators. Meanwhile, prices for nonstaple foods and vegetables also rose. In the first quarter of 1988, prices for nonstaple foods climbed by 24.2 percent, and fresh-vegetable prices rose by 48.7 percent.

As living costs increased, students began to demonstrate again. In the midst of economic and political troubles, however, Zhao Ziyang, under the push of Deng Xiaoping, announced in June the deregulation of retail prices for four types of foods: meat, sugar, eggs, and vegetables. Cigarettes and alcoholic beverages were added to the list in July. News of imminent, sweeping price decontrol—real or rumored—led to panic buying in several cities, including Harbin and Guangzhou.

Showdown in Tiananmen Square

The price deregulations were badly timed. Along with rampant corruption, they fueled discontent among urban residents, especially college students. Another wave of campus disturbances in late 1988 and early 1989 escalated into nationwide student demonstrations following Hu Yaobang's sudden death on April 15, 1989. Student demonstrators marched to Tiananmen Square to place memorial wreaths and demand "correct evaluation" of Hu

Hu Yaobang was popular among young Chinese because of his relatively tolerant stance toward student demonstrations, but this led to his forced resignation as general secretary of the CCP. His sudden death on April 15, 1989, touched off mass demonstrations across the nation, such as this one in Beijing.

Yaobang. They also called for the rehabilitation of all people wrongly persecuted in the campaigns against spiritual pollution and bourgeois liberalization; the publication of the salaries and income sources of all top Party and government leaders and their children; substantially increased stipends, salaries, and budgets for students, teachers, and educational programs; and new legislation promoting freedom of the press and public expression. When their request for a meeting with Premier Li Peng was refused, four student leaders staged a dramatic petition on April 22: in the manner of an imperial petition in traditional China, they knelt on the steps of the Great Hall of the People in Tiananmen Square, where the official memorial service for Hu Yaobang was being performed, holding their scrolled-up demands above their heads.

The response of the Politburo, however, was to refuse to give in to students' demands. At an urgent meeting on April 22, the Politburo decided to terminate the official mourning period for Hu Yaobang; to maintain the original verdict on Hu; and to reaffirm the correctness of the 1987 campaign against bourgeois liberalism.

On April 23, at this critical juncture, Zhao Ziyang left for a scheduled weeklong visit to North Korea. As people of all walks of life, including industrial workers, joined student demonstrators, an enlarged meeting of the Politburo Standing Committee was held on April 25; it described the student protest as "turmoil" (*dongluan* in Chinese). In an editorial printed in the *People's Daily* the following day, Party leaders publicized their tough stand. The editorial blamed "an extremely small number of people" for "flaunting the banner of democracy" to incite students and undermine order in China. "Their purpose," the editorial claimed, "was to sow dissension among the people, plunge the whole country into chaos and sabotage the political situation of stability and unity. This is a planned conspiracy and a disturbance. Its essence is to, once and for all, negate the leadership of the [Communist Party] and the socialist system."

Outraged students responded to the editorial by staging more massive marches on Tiananmen. On April 27, the day following the publication of the *People's Daily* editorial, the number of demonstrators marching to Tiananmen Square doubled—to as many as 100,000. In addition, more than half a million Beijing residents lined the streets of the demonstration route, offering food, drink, and encouragement to the protesters.

Zhao Ziyang adopted a more conciliatory approach upon his return from North Korea at the end of April. After consulting with Deng Xiaoping, Zhao—in a May 4 speech to a meeting of the Asian Development Bank—offered to meet the "reasonable demands of the students" through "democratic and legal means." For a while it seemed that Zhao's conciliatory approach might defuse the volatile situation. By the second week of May, the number of demonstrators in Tiananmen Square began to dwindle noticeably. Student leaders, however, soon discovered a golden opportunity to sustain their movement: the scheduled visit of Soviet leader Mikhail Gorbachev from May 15 to 18.

To grab the attention of the international media and dramatize their call for democratic reforms, several hundred students began a sit-in and hunger strike in Tiananmen Square on May 13. As the situation intensified, Zhao and Deng began to diverge. Zhao proposed to further soften the government's stand, while Deng was determined to get tough with the students. During his talk with Gorbachev on May 16, a frustrated Zhao revealed that Deng held ultimate power, indirectly pointing the finger at the old man for the chaos. Once Gorbachev was out of the country, martial law in Beijing was declared on May 19 over the objection of Zhao Ziyang, who subsequently disappeared from the political stage.

When troops attempted to clear Tiananmen Square in late May, they were unexpectedly blocked by students and residents of Beijing. After a two-week-long stalemate, Deng Xiaoping decided on harsh

A lone Chinese man blocks a column of tanks at the entrance to Tiananmen Square on June 5, 1989—the morning after Chinese troops violently dispersed a group of pro-democracy students who had been protesting in the square since mid-April. For many observers this video image instantly defined the struggle between the Communist Party and the people of China.

measures to put an end to the pro-democracy demonstrations. On June 3, 1989, units of the People's Liberation Army, backed by tanks and armored personnel carriers, began to converge on Tiananmen Square. Beijing residents attempting to block the soldiers' routes to the square were fired on, and an unknown number were killed. By the early-morning hours of June 4, the army had forced its way into Tiananmen Square and surrounded the students on three sides. Precisely what happened next is difficult to ascertain, but several recent examinations by China scholars and media organizations in the West suggest that few students were actually killed inside Tiananmen Square—despite early reports of a massacre of up to 2,000 there. Rather, the recent accounts indicate that the student demonstrators withdrew from the square sometime before dawn on June 4, and it was in the surrounding streets and in neighborhoods around Beijing that the army killed students and other citizens in a number of clashes. The actual death toll will probably never be known, but estimates range from about 800 to more than 2,000.

Chinese president Hu Jintao (left) welcomes South Korean president Roh Moo-Hyun to Beijing. After taking office in 2003, Hu presided over a decade of robust economic growth.

A Rising Power in the 21st Century

On June 9, less than a week after the crackdown at Tiananmen Square, Deng met with leaders of martial law troops. In his speech, he reminded the new leadership that the official policy of "one center, two basic points" that had been adopted at the Thirteenth Party Congress was correct, and reform and opening up should be continued. "Not a single word should be changed to the political report of the Thirteenth Party Congress," Deng admonished his audience, present or not.

Five months later, he wrote a letter to the CCP Central Committee, asking to step down from his last position in the Party as chairman of the Central Military Commission (CMC). He told those colleagues who had tried to persuade him to stay on, "I have made up my mind, period. If I have done nothing else for the party, at least I will set this precedent of voluntary retirement."

Deng's choice for the position of CCP general secretary was Jiang Zemin (b. 1926), former Party secretary of Shanghai. In order to make sure that Jiang had the political clout to carry out his policies, Deng designated Jiang as the core of a "third generation" of Party leadership and, in November 1989, passed on his position of CMC chairman to Jiang. To forestall doubts about Jiang's ability to lead the People's Liberation Army—Jiang had no military experience whatsoever—Deng reasoned, "Jiang is well qualified to be chairman of the Central Military Commission because he is well qualified to be general secretary of the Party."

But very soon, Deng himself would have doubts about Jiang's abilities as general secretary of the Party. Instead of vigorously promoting economic reform and further opening up China to the outside world, as Deng had hoped, Jiang took a more cautious

Deng Xiaoping selected Jiang Zemin (left) and Zhu Rongji (right) to continue his program of reforms during the 1990s.

approach. He became involved in the conservative debate on the nature of reforms and voiced the conservative themes of retrenchment over growth, and state planning over a market-based economy. As a result, China's economic growth slowed between 1989 and 1991.

Pushing the Reform Agenda Forward

Deng Xiaoping, officially retired though by no means completely out of politics, was disappointed at the conservative resurgence and the stagnation of the reforms he had set in motion. In early 1991 he published, under a pen name, a series of four pro-reform commentaries in *Liberation Daily*, the Party newspaper in Shanghai. He also managed to promote a reformist, Zhu Rongji (b. 1928), to the post of vice-premier in April 1991.

In August of that year, however, a coup attempt was launched against the Soviet Union's reform-minded leader, Mikhail Gorbachev. Though the coup collapsed within three days, the Soviet Communist Party quickly lost power and legitimacy, and by the end of the year the Soviet Union had broken apart. In China, conservative leaders viewed this as a cautionary tale and took a tougher stand against reform and reformers.

But Deng believed that China's reform policies needed to go forward. Between January 18 and February 21, 1992, he visited the special economic zones in Shenzhen and Zhuhai and elsewhere in the south. During these visits (later known as the "southern tour"), Deng emphasized the importance for China's development of economic reform and opening up to the world. Without the reform and opening up that began in 1979, he argued, the CCP would not have survived the Tiananmen Square unrest 10 years later, and China would have disintegrated into civil war. Similarly, Deng said, China would reach a dead end in its development without continued reform and opening up in the future. The basic line of "one center, two basic points," in Deng's words, "should be [China's] policy line for the next one hundred years."

Pushed along by Deng, Jiang Zemin belatedly jumped on the bandwagon of reform and opening up. He delivered a speech at the Central Party School on June 9, openly endorsing Deng's reformist themes, and reiterated Deng's ideas in the political report to the Fourteenth Party Congress in October. With reform back to the center of the CCP's policy, Deng strengthened Jiang's position by abolishing the Central Advisory Commission and removing several opponents from military leadership positions. Meanwhile, he also chose Jiang's eventual successor, Hu Jintao. A new round of reform and opening up followed.

With Deng's support, Jiang gradually came into his own as a political leader. After he was made president of China in 1993, he consolidated his power by purging Chen Xitong (b. 1930), Party secretary of Beijing and a Politburo member, in 1995 and by removing Qiao Shi (b. 1924), chairman of the Standing Committee of the National People's Congress and a standing member of the Politburo, in 1997. He purged Chen because of the latter's alleged involvement in corruption and removed Qiao through retirement. After the death of Deng Xiaoping in February 1997, Jiang became the most powerful man in China, with three impressive titles: general secretary, chairman of the CMC, and president of the People's Republic of China. He had the honor of administering the transfer of Hong Kong from Britain to China in 1997 and the return of Macao from Portugal to China in 1999.

In February 2000 Jiang Zemin introduced a new political theory dubbed the "three represents": that the Chinese Communist Party has always represented the most advanced productive forces (now this refers to the so-called red capitalists, owners of private enterprises who have been permitted to join the Party), the most advanced culture, and the fundamental interests of the broadest masses of the Chinese people (instead of workers and peasants, as defined previously). The theory was incorporated into the newly amended constitution of the CCP (and later into the constitution of the People's Republic of China) as a guideline for the work of the Party, along with Marxism-Leninism, Mao Zedong Thought, and Deng Xiaoping Theory.

Under the masterful management of Zhu Rongji, China's economy experienced rapid and stable growth in the period 1992–2002 and survived the Asian financial crisis of 1997, which devastated the economies of many of China's prosperous neighbors. China also adopted a new strategy to promote economic growth in the traditionally underdeveloped western part of the country, streamlined central and local bureaucracies, and carried out state-enterprise reforms.

But perhaps the most significant economic development in China around the turn of the 21st century was the country's entry into the World Trade Organization (WTO). The WTO is a global organization that sets the rules of trade among its nearly 150 member states. After more than a dozen years of difficult negotiations—including opposition from the United States, some of it based on outrage at the Tiananmen Square crackdown—China was formally accepted as a full member of the WTO in 2001. This signaled China's integration into the world economy, led to a large increase in foreign investment, and solidified China's commitment to a more market-based economy. It also opened up new opportunities for China's continued economic growth.

Into the 21st Century: Changes and Challenges

Thanks to the economic reform and opening up policies initiated by Deng Xiaoping, China has experienced momentous changes since the late 1970s. China's gross domestic product (GDP)—the total value of goods and services produced in the country annually, a primary measure of economic performance—quadrupled between 1980 and 1995. More important, between 1980 and 1997, GDP per capita (GDP divided by population) also quadrupled—meaning that Chinese citizens overall are considerably better off than they were a generation ago. Indeed, some experts believe that as many as 600 million Chinese have been lifted out of poverty since the beginning of Deng's reforms. China's economic expansion—growth rates averaged an amazing 9.5 percent annually between 1978 and 2010, according to Chinese government statistics—is unprecedented. But that is only part of the story. China's economic structure has also been transformed from a centrally planned economy to a market economy. As the share of state enterprises' output in the economy has declined—from more than 80 percent in 1978 to about 40 percent in 2011—the private sector, almost nonexistent in the late 1970s, has emerged to become a dominant and dynamic force.

Less well recognized are changes in the political realm. Village leaders, who were once appointed by their superiors in the county government, have since the 1990s been chosen through popular elections. How competitive these elections actually are remains an open question. Before getting on the ballot, candidates are vetted by Communist Party officials. Still, village elections give Chinese citizens a chance to register their displeasure with local leaders.

In the early years of the 21st century, some outside observers—and even a few voices from within the CCP—suggested that competitive village elections signaled that China was on a path to gradual, bottom-up democratization. Today, there appears to be little evidence to support that belief. The CCP continues to assert its exclusive right to rule China, and Party leaders have not demonstrated any inclination to allow popular elections above the village or, in a few cases, township level.

The CCP did achieve a significant political milestone in November 2002, when, at the Sixteenth Party Congress, the first peaceful, institutionalized succession in the history of the People's Republic of China took place. At that time Jiang Zemin stepped down as general secretary and Hu Jintao (b. 1942) succeeded him. In March 2003 Hu was also elected president of the PRC at the First Session of the Tenth National People's Congress. Hu, along with Premier Wen Jiabao (b. 1942) and Vice Premier Wu Yi (b. 1938), has made efforts to burnish the Party's image among China's people. Hu asked the media to pay more attention to the masses instead of to government leaders, ordered government leaders to work on behalf of the people instead of themselves, and abolished the Politburo's annual summer retreat at the beach resort of Beidaihe in Hebei Province.

Despite these and other efforts, popular anger at government policies and pervasive corruption in the CCP appears to be on the rise. In 2010, according to Sun Liping, a professor at China's Tsinghua University, China experienced 180,000 protests, riots, and other mass demonstrations. That comes to nearly 500 incidents per day.

Still, social unrest doesn't yet appear to pose a threat to Communist Party rule. Protesters understand that the CCP doesn't brook direct challenges to its authority, so they stop short of demanding funda-

Hong Kong residents march to protest the growing gap between the wealthy and the poor in China, July 1, 2011. The government allows residents of this semiautonomous city certain freedoms not available to other Chinese, including the right to hold public protests.

mental political change. For his 2008 book *Out of Mao's Shadow*, journalist Philip Pan interviewed leaders of a massive workers' protest that rocked the city of Liaoyang in 2002. The protest leaders, Pan reported, recognized that as long as China's authoritarian political system remained intact,

> those with positions of power could always abuse it, and workers could hope only for marginal improvements in their lives. For real progress, [the protest leaders] thought democratic reform was necessary, and they believed that most workers supported such a goal. But they also knew that persuading workers to participate in a protest advocating democratic change would be all but impossible. The workers had internalized the lessons of the Tiananmen massacre. Everybody knew that the party would quickly crush a direct challenge to its authority, and nobody wanted to go to prison. People were too afraid.

While they remain willing to crush protests if necessary, CCP leaders have also recognized the need to address the sources of popular resentment. In 2011, for instance, President Hu Jintao issued a warning to Communist Party members on the occasion of the 90th anniversary of the CCP's founding. "Corruption," Hu said, "will cost the party the support and trust of the people."

Other shortcomings and failures could also cost the CCP the support and trust of the people. Any serious and prolonged setback to China's economy could undermine the Party's justification for its monopoly on power. China's leaders must therefore keep the economy growing at a brisk pace. They must address growing income inequality. While entrepreneurs, children of high-ranking officials ("princelings"), officials-turned-businesspeople, and other groups have accumulated substantial fortunes from China's economic growth, peasants and employees of state enterprises have largely been left behind. The "floating population"—rural residents who have migrated to China's cities in search of work—presents another significant problem in urban and economic planning. According to official Chinese statistics, the floating population reached a staggering 211 million in 2009.

On the international stage, there is little doubt that China has arrived as a major player. But with growing global influence comes an array of challenges. Perhaps most significant is how to manage the bilateral relationship with the United States. The economic and strategic interests of these two nations won't always coincide. Friction over economic issues periodically bubbled up after the world financial crisis of 2008. And analysts almost universally interpreted President Barack Obama's 2011 decision to establish a permanent U.S. military presence in Australia as a response to Chinese provocations in the South China Sea.

★ ★ ★ ★ ★

China has indeed come a long way in the past 160 years. After suffering a century of foreign interference, during which the once-proud empire degenerated into a semi-colonial state, China emerged after World War II to shed foreign domination. Yet the first quarter century after the establishment of the People's Republic of China was filled with economic setbacks, social disruption, and political repression—all of which stifled progress. With the introduction of economic reforms in the late 1970s, China began to forge a new path, and two and a half decades later this giant of Asia is an economic dynamo that stands on the verge of becoming one of the world's most influential powers. But while progress has been dramatic, it has also been uneven, and China has a long way to go before all its people can enjoy the fruits of modernity.

Chronology

1839 Commissioner Lin Zexu arrives in Guangzhou to ban the opium trade.

1840 The Opium War officially breaks out between Great Britain and China in January.

1842 The Treaty of Nanjing is signed on August 29, bringing the Opium War to an end.

1856 Anglo-French forces resume military actions at the city of Guangzhou and start another war against China.

1858 In June the Treaties of Tianjin are signed with Russia, the United States, Britain, and France.

1860 In October British soldiers burn the Summer Palace (Yuan Ming Yuan) to the ground; the Conventions of Beijing are signed to end the war between the Anglo-French alliance and China.

1861 The Self-Strengthening Movement begins.

1884–85 The Sino-French War is fought over Annam (now Vietnam).

1894–95 The Sino-Japanese War is fought.

1898 The reform movement led by Emperor Guangxu lasts 103 days.

1900 The Boxer uprising occurs.

1901 The Boxer Protocol is signed on September 7.

1911–12 The Chinese Revolution under Sun Zhongshan is successful; Emperor Xuantong (Puyi) abdicates, and the Qing dynasty falls.

1919 The May Fourth Movement occurs to protest the terms of the Versailles Treaty and pro-Japanese sentiments.

1921 The Chinese Communist Party (CCP) is founded in July.

1927 The Guomindang (GMD) government is established in Nanjing.

1931 On September 18 a bomb (probably planted by Japanese soldiers) explodes along the Japanese-operated Southern Manchurian Railway; Japan uses incident as a pretext to conquer Manchuria.

1934–35 The Long March occurs.

1936 Jiang Jieshi is placed under house arrest after a mutiny breaks out in Xi'an on December 12; a united front against the Japanese is formed between the CCP and the GMD.

1937 Japanese troops invade China, touching off the struggle the Chinese refer to as the Anti-Japanese War.

1945 The Japanese surrender to the Allies to end World War II.

1949 The People's Republic of China is founded on October 1.

1950–53 The Korean War is fought.

1958–61 The Great Leap Forward, an attempt at rapid industrialization, is carried out, with disastrous consequences.

1966 The Cultural Revolution begins in May; Liu Shaoqi and Deng Xiaoping are dismissed from office.

1971 Lin Biao dies.

1973 Deng Xiaoping returns to power as vice premier, PLA chief of staff, and a member of the Politburo.

1976 Zhou Enlai dies on January 8; Deng Xiaoping is once again dismissed in April; Mao Zedong dies on September 9; the Gang of Four is arrested in October, and the Cultural Revolution ends.

1977 Deng Xiaoping returns to power in July.

1979 China and the United States establish full diplomatic relations on January 1.

1989 In the midst of pro-democracy protests in Beijing's Tiananmen Square, martial law is declared in May; in June army units force their way into Tiananmen Square and disperse the protesters, an unknown number of whom are killed; Zhao Ziyang is removed from his post as general secretary of the CCP, and Jiang Zemin replaces him; in November, Deng Xiaoping retires.

1992 Deng Xiaoping conducts his "southern tour" in support of economic reforms.

1993 Jiang Zemin is elected president of the People's Republic of China.

1997 Deng Xiaoping dies in February, aged 92.

1999 During a bombing campaign to stop Serbian aggression in Kosovo, bombs dropped from a U.S. warplane hit the Chinese embassy in Belgrade, spurring outrage in China; later in the year the United States and China reach agreement regarding China's entry into the World Trade Organization (WTO).

2000 Jiang Zemin introduces the "three represents" theory.

2001 A Chinese F-8 fighter plane collides with an American E-P3 surveillance plane off the coast of Hainan, causing tensions between the respective governments; China officially becomes a member of the WTO.

2002 In November, Hu Jintao is elected general secretary of the CCP at the 16th Party Congress in Beijing; Jiang Zemin remains chairman of the Central Military Commission.

2003 Hu Jintao is elected president of the People's Republic of China; China successfully mounts its first manned space mission.

2005 China invites James Soong, head of the Taiwan's People First Party, to tour the mainland, marking a change in strategy in the country's effort to reclaim Taiwan.

2009 According to official government statistics, China's "floating population" of migrant workers reaches 211 million.

2010 China claims as territorial waters the entire South China Sea; according to a Chinese scholar, some 180,000 protests, riots, and mass demonstrations occur throughout China over the course of the year.

2011 President Hu Jintao issues a public warning to members of the CCP about the dangers of corruption; the United States announces the establishment of a permanent American military presence in Australia, a move generally interpreted as an effort to counterbalance Chinese expansion in the South China Sea.

Glossary

big-character poster—a large-format poster hung in a public place, for the purpose of political communication or protest.

cadre—in China, an official of the government, usually a member of the Chinese Communist Party.

cat theory—a pragmatic thought about economic activities attributed to Deng Xiaoping, who said, "Black cat, white cat; it is a good cat if it catches mice."

cult of personality—the tendency to treat a leader (particularly a Communist leader) as an impeccable deity instead of a fallible human being.

four cardinal principles—guiding principles of the Chinese Communist Party, introduced by Deng Xiaoping: adherence to the socialist road, the people's democratic dictatorship, Communist Party leadership, and Marxism-Leninism–Mao Zedong Thought.

Four Modernizations—the goal of China's economic development strategy, announced in 1975 and to be achieved by the end of 20th century, involving the four areas of agriculture, industry, national defense, and science and technology.

household responsibility system—a system of production in agriculture in which households take the responsibility for producing.

memorial—a formal written presentation from an imperial government official to the emperor.

Mao Zedong Thought—the school of socialist thought named after Mao Zedong and long accepted as the governing ideology of the Chinese Communist Party, which consists of a combination of Marxist theory and Chinese practice.

"one country, two systems"—the idea proposed by Deng Xiaoping for unifying parts of China with different social and economic systems by which two different social and economic systems (socialism and capitalism) coexist in one country (China).

Politburo—the most important decision-making body of the CCP Central Committee, consisting of between 15 and 33 people who are elected from full Central Committee members; its Standing Committee, consisting of between 5 and 10 people, is the most powerful.

revisionism—a tendency to revise the orthodox policies of such leaders as Stalin and Mao Zedong.

special administrative regions—regions reunited with China and governed on the basis of the principle of "one country, two systems"; Hong Kong Special Administrative Region and Macao Special Administrative Region were established in 1997 and 1999, respectively.

special economic zones—cities designated by the CCP to attract direct foreign investment and promote exports; the four special economic zones—Shenzhen, Zhuhai, Shantou, and Xiamen—were established in 1979.

tael—one ounce of silver; a unit of exchange (most importantly, a unit of tax payment made to government treasuries) in imperial China.

thought reform—an extensive period of ideological training designed to "correct" the supposedly erroneous thinking of Chinese intellectuals with bourgeois backgrounds.

Further Reading

Fewsmith, Joseph. *China Since Tiananmen: The Politics of Transition*. New York: Cambridge University Press, 2001.

Gilley, Bruce. *Tiger on the Brink: Jiang Zemin and China's New Elite*. Berkeley: University of California Press, 1998.

Jin, Qiu. *The Culture of Power: The Lin Biao Incident in the Cultural Revolution*. Stanford, Calif.: Stanford University Press, 1999.

Kissinger, Henry. *Henry Kissinger on China*. New York: Penguin, 2012.

Lampton, David M. *Same Bed, Different Dreams: Managing U.S.-China Relations 1989–2000*. Berkeley: University of California Press, 2001.

Lieberthal, Kenneth. *Governing China: From Revolution Through Reform*. 2nd ed. New York: W. W. Norton & Co., 2004.

Pan, Philip P. *Out of Mao's Shadow: The Struggle for the Soul of a New China*. New York: Simon & Schuster, 2008.

Spence, Jonathan D. *The Search for Modern China*. New York: W. W. Norton & Co., 1999.

Terrill, Ross. *Mao: A Biography*. Stanford, Calif.: Stanford University Press, 1999.

Wang, James C. F. *Contemporary Chinese Politics: An Introduction*. 7th ed. Englewood Cliffs, N.J.: Prentice Hall, 2001.

Wasserstrom, Jeffrey N. *China in the 21st Century: What Everyone Needs to Know*. New York: Oxford University Press USA, 2010.

Yang, Benjamin. *Deng: A Political Biography*. Armonk, N.Y.: M. E. Sharpe, 1998.

Internet Resources

http://english.peopledaily.com.cn/

English-language version of the *People's Daily*, China's most important official newspaper.

http://chinadaily.com.cn/en

Website of *China Daily*, a Chinese newspaper in English.

http://www.hoover.org/publications/china-leadership-monitor

China Leadership Monitor is a web-based journal with articles by eminent scholars in the United States on China's leadership.

http://www.china.org.cn

Information on political, social, economic, and cultural life in China.

http://www.chinaknowledge.org/History/history.htm

This site provides an overview of the Qing dynasty in China and includes links to other periods of history in China as well as information on other aspects of China.

Index

Numbers in ***bold italics*** refer to captions.

Picture Credits

Contributors

DR. ZHIYUE BO is Associate Professor and chair of the Department of International Studies at St. John Fisher College in Rochester, New York. He obtained a Bachelor of Law and a Master of Law in International Politics from Beijing University and a Ph.D. in Political Science from the University of Chicago. He is widely published in the areas of Chinese politics and history, with articles appearing in such journals as *Journal of Contemporary China, Issues & Studies, Provincial China, Asian Profile, Journal of Chinese Political Science, Chinese Social Sciences Review,* and *Chinese Law & Government.* He has also served as a guest editor for both *Chinese Law & Government* and *Journal of Contemporary China.* His most recent book is *Chinese Provincial Leaders: Economic Performance and Political Mobility Since 1949* (Armonk, N.Y.: M.E. Sharpe, 2002).

JIANWEI WANG, a native of Shanghai, received his B.A. and M.A in international politics from Fudan University in Shanghai and his Ph.D. in political science from the University of Michigan. He is now the Eugene Katz Letter and Science Distinguished Professor and chair of the Department of Political Science at the University of Wisconsin–Stevens Point. He is also a guest professor at Fudan University in Shanghai and Zhongshan University in Guangzhou.

Professor Wang's teaching and research interests focus on Chinese foreign policy, Sino-American relations, Sino-Japanese relations, East Asia security affairs, UN peacekeeping operations, and American foreign policy. He has published extensively in these areas. His most recent publications include *Power of the Moment: America and the World After 9/11* (Xinhua Press, 2002), which he coauthored, and *Limited Adversaries: Post-Cold War Sino-American Mutual Images* (Oxford University Press, 2000).

Wang is the recipient of numerous awards and fellowships, including grants from the MacArthur Foundation, Social Science Research Council, and Ford Foundation. He has also been a frequent commentator on U.S.-China relations, the Taiwan issue, and Chinese politics for major news outlets.